Pacesetting for Christ-Centered Living

Pacesetting
for
Christ-Centered Living
A Transformational Journey

Philemon Nfor

ISBN: 979-8-9923580-1-8

Copyright: 2025 by Philemon Nfor

All rights reserved

No portion of this book may be reproduced in any form without written permission from the publisher or author, except as permitted by U.S. copyright law.

KLG Press

Scripture marked (NIV) taken from THE HOLY BIBLE, NEW INTERNATIONAL VERSION ®, NIV © 1973, 1975, 1984, 2011 by Biblica, Inc.® Used by permission. All rights reserved worldwide.

Scripture quotations marked NLT are taken from the *Holy Bible*, New Living Translation, © 1996, 2004, 2015 by Tyndale House Foundation. Used by permission of Tyndale House Publishers, Inc. Carol Stream, Illinois 60188. All rights reserved.

Scripture quotations taken from the Amplified ® Bible (AMP), Copyright © 2015 by The Lockman Foundation. Used by permission. Lockman.org

Scripture quotations marked RSV are from Revised Standard Version of the Bible, copyright © 1946,1952, and 1971. National Council of the Churches of Christ in the United States of America. Used by permission. All rights reserved worldwide.

Scripture taken from the New King James Version (NKJV) © Copyright © 1982 by Thomas Nelson. Used by permission. All rights reserved.

To Jim~

*Whose desire to make me excel
in leadership formation was cut short by
the circumstances of life and God's decision.*

Preface

Pastor Philemon Nfor has always stood out for the quality and originality of the texts he offers his readers. His writings reveal a characteristic depth that reflects both epistemological rigor and a well-structured general and theological culture. I have often engaged with the meditations he publishes daily on the digital forums we share with great attention. The precision in his choice of words, the simplicity of his syntax, the maturity of his style, and the brilliance of the themes he addresses are among the elements that give Reverend Nfor's texts a luminosity that sets them apart from many other texts on the evangelical market. In this publication, *Pacesetting for Christ-Centered Living,* the same author returns with a sharper lucidity and a maturity that has acquired more wisdom to lead us on a journey to the summit of holistic transformation.

The structure of the text, as presented in the summary and by the book's subtitle, "100 Days for a Transformational Journey," promises the reader a joyful adventure at the heart of an interaction with Christ with a view to complete metamorphosis. Beyond metamorphosis, I would speak of transfiguration in view of the different dimensions and different human faculties that this text aims to transform. And this is the first merit of this work: its vocation to bring about positive changes in the reader's life. It should be noted here that the journey proposed by Pastor Nfor is structured around thirty-two stations, each carefully articulated around a theme of awakening, edification, and/or enlightenment that speaks to the reader's soul. From the theme of "Adoration," which is the fundamental basis of human life and the first station on this journey, to the great existential question, "When Time Dies, Where Will You Be," which is the last stage of the journey, it passes through a thousand and one other themes, including "Blessed and Blessing, Caring & Comfort, Character Building, and God's Plan." Philemon Nfor methodically guides his reader on a path of fascinating and moving discoveries that transport the reader to a revelation of self, nature, and God. This is precisely the second merit of this publication: the author's ability to weave a text of a methodological and heuristic nature. The reader makes no effort to discover and understand the different spheres of life presented by the author. This is a quality of the author that should be praised in its proper proportion.

I would now like to say a few words about the content of the text and point out that the substance that shaped this book is truly the nectar of God. You drink it down to the dregs, and just when you think the cup is empty, the liquid rises again, revealing that you are in contact with an inexhaustible source, such is the depth of Pastor Nfor's writings. Reading through the chapter on worship, the reader quickly realizes that science and faith, which appear to be contradictory, are in fact close cousins that complement each other at the highest level. Philemon Nfor suggests that science is a tool in the service of worship. Scientific discoveries through knowledge of the laws of nature, knowledge of the stars and planets, knowledge of the functioning of the human body and other things reveal the Greatness, Majesty, Wisdom, and Magnificence of God, the Creator of heaven and earth and all that it contains. It is through discoveries and inventions that man better understands the depths of the Creator, God. Science therefore offers human and Christian faith the material for worship because it tells us who God is. The mastery with which Pastor Nfor analyzes this theme of worship is symptomatic of the spirit that governs all the analyses in the book. The relevance of these analyses demonstrates our author's third merit: his ability to delve deeply into the subjects he addresses. He dissects the biblical text.

Regarding the author's style, I stated at the beginning of my remarks that it exudes exemplary maturity. Philemon Nfor's style is heavily dominated by metaphors and allegories. He makes very consistent use of images in the manner of Christ, particularly when speaking of parables. Each of Philemon Nfor's daily experiences is a divine message that can serve as a parable or allegory for his audience. This allows us to better grasp the very essence of life and walking with Christ. It is this style that makes his various messages throughout the book so relevant and compelling. What I will not omit in this commentary is the spiritual dimension that overshadows all the merits of this book. Pastor Nfor's pen is simply guided by the Spirit. His text pierces the reader's soul to reach the depths of their heart.

Reading *Pacesetting for Christ-Centered Living* by Philemon Nfor, is truly sowing and reaping in the field of the good master, an inspired and inspiring book.

Rev. Dr. Jean Libom Li Likeng

President of the African Evangelical Alliance;

President of the Alliance of Evangelicals, Cameroon.

Acknowledgement

A piece of work like this book contains is the product of many minds and influences over the years. Christ-centered living is a journey I have been taking since 1981 when Rev. Joseph Kindefor took his time to disciple me and give me baby steps into the faith. My deep appreciation goes to him. I also thank God for all the pastors and men of God who have shaped my life; for the disciples I have had in life who have made me stay focused as I worked on their spirituality, and for close ministry friends who have been my partners in the journey of life. Among them, I greatly appreciate Elder Edward Ndzi who showed me gracious presence at some tough moments when I needed a shoulder to lean on.

As far as my journey in pacesetting for various aspects of the Christ life is concerned, I sincere appreciate Justice Prudence Galega who catalyzed the writing of the *Pacesetters* and ensured that I did not stop for any reason. I also appreciate Mme Nformi Joan who started editing my early writings when my language was nothing to write home about. He gave it meaning and gave me assurance that I could write even better. As for Pastor Karen Garrison who has taken the pains of sorting out the particular devotionals to publish and working out its publication, I can only say, for lack of better words in English, thank you very much.

For my wife Rose, and the children, thank you for being there in the good times and the bad, helping me to navigate the spiritual detours and remaining in the path of divine guidance that has resulted in this product. Above all, all praise and glory go to God whose Name is to be glorified in the transformations that this work will produce.

Table Of Contents

Adoration

He Holds All Things Together: Worship Him	17
Adore The God Who Makes the Difference in Life!	20
Worship The Sovereign, Loving and Just God!	23

Immutable

Your God Is Ageless	26
Celebrate Your Ageless God	30
Celebrate The Lord Your Bracer	32

Family Of God

You Are God's	34
Christian: God Is Celebrating You	36
Can God Use You to Help?	38
Do Not Exploit, Explore!	41

Omnipresent

God Will Hear You!	44
God Is There Always: For You!	46
The Lord Shall Come To Your Rescue!	49

Blessed & Blessing

You Are Special!	52
Your Lord Will Provide: Honor Him With It	56
Hate No One!	59
Seek His Blessing Always	62

Caring & Comfort

Leave It All to Him!	65

It Is Not About Their Strength or Yours!	67
He Is The Lord of All Age Groups!	70
God Will Care for You to Your Old Age!	72
Your Burden Bearer!	75
The Greatest Comfort Is in Knowing God!	77

Purpose & Plans

Nothing Is New to God	79
Different Problems: Same God!	82
The Way to Greatness Is Death!	85
What Do You Have: Vision or Fantasy?	88

God's Beauty

May The Lord Grow and Glow Your Heart!	92
What God, What Me!	95
Enjoy The Beauty of God	98

Creator & Creation

Celebrate the Creator of Nature	101
Worship The God of Beauty!	103
Human Life Is Worthy!	106

Deliverance & Care

Your God Will Arise!	109

Character Building

The God of Firm but Loving Rebuke!	111
Live As to Be Honored	113

Faithfulness & Provision

When You Pass Through the Water and Fire!	115
Let The Righteous Celebrate His Justice!	118
Faithfulness: The Best Way to Promotion!	120

The Lord Will Hear You!	122

Generosity

Worship Your Giving God!	124
Philanthropy or Generosity?	126
What Is Guiding Your Giving?	131
Do Not Eat Without Sowing	134

Jehovah-Jireh

Let God Give You Life!	137

Love

Celebrate God as Love	140
Social Capital Is Invested Not Exploited!	144
Do Not Throw At, Reach Out To	147
Overcoming Hurt to Care!	150
More than Rules: Relate!	153

God's Guidance

Touch the Earth from Heaven!	157
Just Follow and You Will Be Fine!	160
God Is Your Ever-Present Guide!	162
Let God Lead	164

God's Plans

Celebrate He Who Has the Final Say	167
God Has the Plan: Follow Him!	169
Celebrate Your Builder!	172

God Of Possibilities

Your God Shall Provide for You!	174
Dare With Your Able God!	177
Live In the Realm of Possibilities!	180

Christian Life

Let God Prepare You!	184
Be Pushful to Be Useful!	187
Sacrifice Is Not A Waste	190

Christian Protection

Be Not Shattered: They Gather to Scatter!	192
Be Focused Not Surprised!	195

Provision & Obedience

Go: He Will Meet Your Needs!	198
Learn To Listen	201
Wisdom Is Not Only Learned in School	204

Wisdom

Christ Is Our Wisdom	207
Wisdom Is for Daily Usefulness	210
Seek Wisdom for Your Life!	212
Edify and Expose Didactically	214

Grace & Mercy

Worship The God of Conviction	217
Worship The Righteous God	220
Problem: When Honor Is Demanded	223
Live by His Grace and Love	225
His Grace Is Abundant	228

Fellowship

Have a Great Fellowship	230
Relationships Are Built, Not Picked!	233

Relationships

Social Relationships: 　Between Numbers & Quantity!	236

Celebrate The God Of Relationships	239
Confront Your Progress Blockers!	242
Giving	
Giving Is Impactful Investment!	245
Selflessly Insist on Doing What Is Right	247
Build and Be Built	250
Value Giving Beyond Today	252
Pride & Humility	
In Humility You Can Listen!	255
Hard Times Can Be Treasure Times Too!	257
Praise & Celebration	
Let the Music Play On	260
Please The Greatest Pleasure Giver!	263
Service	
Serve to Save Lives!	266
Commitment Makes Every Age Meaningful!	269
Do Not Just Live to "Make It" in Life	271
Truth & Self-Control	
Life Is Not a Game	273
Live by Grace and Truth	276
Wealth	
When Wealth Breeds Pride!	279
Worship God With Your Wealth!	282
Celebrate The Lord of Your Harvest	286
Wealth for Health and Service	289
Decision	
When Time Dies, Where Will You Be?	292

Adoration

Day 1 *Adoration*
HE HOLDS ALL THINGS TOGETHER: WORSHIP HIM!

Have you ever had the opportunity to get out of your lighted home into the dark and watch the stars in the skies? We often did that in the village when we did not have streetlights. It was interesting to watch the stars seeming to move from one part of the sky to another. Now I know stars do not really move. "This [apparent] motion is due to the Earth's rotation. As the spin of the earth carries us eastward at almost one thousand miles per hour, we see stars rising in the east, passing overhead, and setting in the west. The sun, moon, and planets appear to move across the sky much like the stars."[1] It is the same effect as when you sit in a moving car. The trees seem to move but what moves is the car! The earth is spinning around itself and moving round the sun. Never has it gotten out of orbit! Why? Science?

No! Science can only explain how things happen; it cannot say why they happen. The great scientific discoveries are simply observations. It was in noting that all the things you throw into the air come back down that Isaac Newton concluded that there is a force on the ground that pulls downwards. He called it gravity. He did not bring gravity

---
[1] https://brainly.com/question/21481150

about. He discovered it. The pride of science is like the annoying pride of the Europeans who "discovered Africa and America" and speak about it as if those places did not exist before they "discovered" them.

Before the plane could fly, the birds were already in the skies. The first plane only got into the sky in 1903. God has had birds fly for uncounted millennia! Before the ship got to move in the waters, the fish were there.

God holds all things. **"He is before all things, and in him all things hold together" (Colossians 1:17 NIV).** God put the sun in place and gave it enough magnetic force to hold together all the planets. Man cannot even approach the sun, let alone do anything about its magnetism. The earth is 93 million miles (150.92 million km) away from the sun! Yet we are suffering from global warming! What heat! Ah, God! I worship You!

Beloved, when you step out of your door, look up in the sky above and declare like the Psalmist,

"Lord, our Lord, how majestic is your name in all the earth! You have set your glory in the heavens. When I consider your heavens, the work of your fingers, the moon, and the stars, which you have set in place, what is mankind that you are mindful of them, human beings that you care for them?" (Psalm 8:1, 3-4 NIV).

The Lord who has the wisdom to create all these things and hold them in place, has you in His mind, in His heart, in His plans, unto eternity! He even knows you by name!

Ah! How does a human being ignore such care and love from an unfathomable Creator and Sustainer of the universe?

Bow before Him who holds all things. Celebrate His greatness and His wisdom. Magnify Him for His love for you. Above all, trust Him in all situations and be at peace with Him in your life, for as the Bible says in **Romans 11:36 NIV, "… from him and through him and for him are all things. To him be the glory forever! Amen."**

Day 2 *Adoration*

ADORE THE GOD
WHO MAKES THE GREATEST DIFFERENCE IN LIFE!

The village was in an uproar and confusion, wondering if it was a dream! A second village head had just been crowned because the first was found unworthy of the position. He had proven to be selfish and was also selling the land and dispossessing the villagers of their landed property. It was obvious his dethronement would bring greater chaos, so he was simply shifted aside and a faithful person given the leadership responsibility.

A few years later, on the other side of the river, across the boundary was a shout of celebration and great joy. A long-sought-for village head had been crowned and proved to be quite sacrificial and loving towards his village. His presence brought order, peace and unity, and his commitment to the well-being of the villagers brought full satisfaction. He was adored! You see, there is a natural, built-in reality in the heart of man to be repulsed towards what is bad but to rejoice, without a request, to what is great, good and helpful. If, therefore, there is a reason to celebrate and it does not happen, it must be that the good news is not recognized for what it is. God is the Greatest Being in the universe who makes the greatest difference in all life situations. He is most worthy of our adoration.

God can indeed turn things around in favor of those who express faith in Him.

"On the thirteenth day of the twelfth month, the month of Adar, the edict commanded by the king was to be carried out. On this day the enemies of the Jews had hoped to overpower them, but now the tables were turned and the Jews got the upper hand over those who hated them" (Esther 9:1 NIV).

God, in response to the prayers of the Jews, turned things around and the impact on the nation was great. How would the Jews react to it? The Jews got their total victory on the fourteenth day of the month.

"Mordecai recorded these events, and he sent letters to all the Jews throughout the provinces of King Xerxes, near and far, to have them celebrate annually the fourteenth and fifteenth days of the month of Adar as the time when the Jews got relief from their enemies, and as the month when their sorrow was turned into joy and their mourning into a day of celebration. He wrote them to observe the days as days of feasting and joy and giving presents of food to one another and gifts to the poor" (Esther 9:20-22 NIV).

Their joy was unending! Note that among the things they did on the day of celebration was the giving of gifts to the poor. Worshiping God does not start and end with singing and dancing. Reaching out to the needy, facilitating the course of care and outreach are worthy aspects of adoring God for His perpetual goodness; His continuous work that makes a difference in our daily lives.

Beloved in the Lord, God has taken care of you. He has kept you from the seen and unseen forces of darkness. The least you can do is adore Him, celebrate Him in singing, dancing, prayer, and in participating in taking away someone's pain. Walk through your life with a heart and hand of thanksgiving for the great ways in which God has made your life so much better, and certainly, God will do more, in Jesus' Name.

Day 3   *Adoration*

WORSHIP THE SOVEREIGN, LOVING AND JUST GOD!

It takes faith and understanding to see that God is not unjust, loving and does all things for the good of His people. There is a popular thought nowadays, that it does not make sense to believe that a loving God can send people to a place of torment called hell. But life itself has natural indicators that justice and love can go together. His ability to do all things does not stop human responsibility and its consequences.

We were close friends in secondary (high) school. We ate together many times, sometimes studied together, went on weekends together and even preached together in turns at church from time to time. But the other two young men chose a lifestyle quite different from mine. They were rough and had little or no time to bother about Christianity out of the Sunday service. They did not pay much attention to morality and preferred self-comfort to sacrificial book work. In the end, both fell along the line, did not make it in school and returned to their villages to face a tough life. Did God love them? Yes! But their lifestyle picked the consequences of justice. I remember times when they mocked me for saying "no" to certain things.

God's love does not mean that everything must always go well. If everything going well was the perfect formula of life, one would not talk about a child of one of the greatest, richest and power-wielding people on earth doing drugs! Someone who has been fed with a golden spoon all the time, went to the best schools and had everything needed and desired at her disposal used drugs? Why? Having everything good is not a formula for a great life.

God humbles us in difficulties and failures to call attention to what is right for us to do and to be blessed. A failure to see and adjust what is wrong blinds and sets the stage for significant stagnation and eventual failure. God was angry with false prophets in Israel who cried out that all was well, even when He was making it clear that Israel would go into exile.

"From the least to the greatest, all are greedy for gain; prophets and priests alike, all practice deceit. They dress the wound of my people as though it were not serious. 'Peace, peace,' they say, when there is no peace. Are they ashamed of their detestable conduct? No, they have no shame at all; they do not even know how to blush. So they will fall among the fallen; 'they will be brought down when I punish them,' says the Lord" (Jeremiah 6:13-15 NIV).

Beloved, check the "wounds" in your heart and body; check the wounds of bad relationships within your family; check the wounds created by corruption in your country, and cry out to God in prayer for mercy, with a repentant heart. The sovereign Lord will defend that which belongs to you. The God of justice will punish your waywardness or that of your family and nation. The loving God will mercifully restore the fortunes of the repentant. There is no greater deception than to expect a loving hand of God in "everything going well" with a disobedient and corrupt person or nation. There is no greater source of blessing than in worshipping God with a truthful, sincere heart and clean hands, among a truthful and sincere people. Worship the sovereign Lord in repentance and expectation. His love will respond with a blessing, in Jesus' Name.

Immutable

(Unchanging)

Day 4   *Immutable*

YOUR GOD IS AGELESS!

Aging is an interesting phenomenon. I looked up to my father and would not allow him to move a step without me when I was young. Even when he was hurrying and I could accompany him, I preferred to run as he walked, just to keep him company. It gave me a sense of security. Then the time came when we were friends, almost "colleagues," as we went hunting together. If I was with the dog in one part of the bush looking for the animal, he was on the opposite, attentive, waiting for any animal that would try to run away from the dog. It was fun but also life-sustaining. Before I knew it, my father looked up to me for strength, for assistance, and even for sustenance. Time caught up with him until the day I got the phone call from a doctor, "Philemon, I am sorry, all the internal organs in your father's body are shutting down. I am not sure he has long to live." I was driving but parked on the side of the road, and stood for some time, to take a breath before continuing. I was still standing there when I got the call announcing: "He has died." Age caught up with him and he rested.

There is such a rush and struggle these days, to keep the body *looking* young and healthy. Food supplements, natural products, and sporting exercises have become ways by which people try to prolong their stay on earth. Yet, the time comes for everyone when no amount of wealth, political power or popularity, can take away the frailty and dependency of the "old person." That we are dependent beings is a reality we face at young and old ages. We come to earth weak and dependent; we leave it weak and dependent.

The only being who does not suffer aging is God. The song we sing, "*Ancient of Days*" sees God with the aged-bound human eye. God is timeless! He was there in the beginning! He has always been there! He created the universe and humanity. The earth and everything shall pass away: all the galaxies, planets, moons and stars discovered and yet to be discovered. All human life on earth shall end. What happens after is in God's Hands who is behind all things. All that exists is the work of His Hands. He holds everything. **"Yes, and from ancient days I am he. No one can deliver out of my hand. When I act, who can reverse it?" (Isaiah 43:13 NIV).**

Beloved, there are many implications for the agelessness of God which you can hold in your heart and live with joy.

- He can be fully trusted. He is the Unhelped Helper. He takes care of all, and none takes care of Him. He is the Giver and Sustainer of life and in Him we live and move

and have our being. Trust your un-depending (independent) dependable God.
- Hope in Him. Because He is ageless, His abilities, wisdom, and knowledge are always the same and perfect. As Paul testified,

"Oh, the depth of the riches of the wisdom and knowledge of God! How unsearchable his judgments, and his paths beyond tracing out! 'Who has known the mind of the Lord? Or who has been his counselor? Who has ever given to God, that God should repay them?' For from him and through him and for him are all things. To him be the glory forever! Amen" (Romans 11:33-36 NIV).

Friend in the Lord, sing this Isaac Watts hymn made popular by Martin Luther with a joyful heart:

"O God, our help in ages past,

Our hope for years to come,

Our shelter from the stormy blast,

And our eternal home.

Before the hills in order stood

Or earth received its frame,

From everlasting you are God,

To endless years the same."

Then confess, "Lord I put my trust in you and hope in you; for now and for always." Indeed, the Lord shall keep you, to your old age and grey hair, in Jesus' Name.

Day 5   Immutable

CELEBRATE YOUR AGELESS GOD!

I am blessed to have enjoyed my maternal great-grandmother before she died. I visited her farm and enjoyed sweet sugarcane and ate the cocoyams she roasted on the farm. Of course, I ate her food too. Above all, she gave me advice. Her word of counsel remains in me as a strong guide in life. However, some of her good counsel, generationally, was out of date. Every counsel from my parents who went unto glory over ten years ago, did not consider some challenges of our contemporary days. Great human wisdom is limited in time, space and even applicability at some point. But there is Someone who is all wise, all strong, all knowing; always living, and very contemporary in His counsel. He is the Ancient of Days, Rock of Ages; our Help in ages past, present and future: God Himself. Hallelujah!

He is the God of Adam, Abraham, Jacob (Israel), Moses, and Joshua. He is the God of David, Solomon, Jehoshaphat, and Zerubbabel. He is the Father of our Lord Jesus Christ, the God of Peter, James, John, and Paul. He is the God of Erasmus, Chrysostom, Martin Luther, John Calvin, John Knox, and Martin Luther King Jr. He is the God of Billy Graham, Charles Swindoll, Ravi Zacharias, and Charles Stanley. He is my God, the God of my children and their children after them to the tenth generation. He is your God and the God of your descendants who will fear and honor Him. What a God!

Yes, **"Jesus Christ is the same yesterday and today and forever" (Hebrews 13:8 NIV).**

That is the God I pray you join me celebrating today. He was there for you. He is there for you. He will be there for you. The ever-living and all-knowing God's counsel is always contemporary, always historically correct, and guides to a great future. His word stands uncorrectable, yet relevant in *all* cultures and every situation in time and wherever. In all situations, He is and ever will be sufficient for you and all who will call on Him. He is worthy of our celebration. Celebrate Him, in Jesus' Name.

Day 6   *Immutable*

CELEBRATE THE LORD YOUR BRACER

Where I come from, it used to be popular to have a drying hut on the farm called "kunde." It stood on four or five poles, laid with bamboos so that corn would be spread on it to get dry. A two-sided thatched roof covered the corn from rain. Often, one or two of the poles were eaten by termites, thus, compromising the security of the hut. That is when a bracing pole was added to the weak pole to keep the hut standing. Those bracers were stronger and lasted longer. Sometimes, we need human bracers for our lives. You may depend on some people professionally, within the family, or spiritually to be firm and successful, just to realize that some of those on whom you depend do not have time for you. Others may even turn against you. This is a general problem, but more serious with people striving for truth, justice and freedom.

When Jesus touched people with the truth, **"From this time many of his disciples turned back and no longer followed him" (John 6:66, NIV).** When He was in deep pain just before the crucifixion, the disciples could not even pray with Him, and when His greatest moment of pain came, and Jesus was arrested,

"Then everyone deserted him and fled. A young man, wearing nothing but a linen garment, was following

Jesus. When they seized him, he fled naked, leaving his garment behind" (Mark 14:50-52 NIV).

Danger! Mark ran off naked! But the Lord was with Jesus, and when He died, the Holy Spirit raised Him up. Paul tells us that at his first defense, everyone deserted him, but the Lord stood with Him and gave him victory. Jesus and Paul had an unfailing bracer; the Lord their God and your God!

Beloved in the Lord, God has promised never to leave nor forsake you.

- When your trusted ones are gone and your life seems drained and lonely,
- When your strength is gone and no one seems to care for your pain,
- When you seem to be drowning in the lake of fiercely opposing powers,
- When it seems as if the best thing for you is to give up, but you have a duty to fulfill to God and humanity,
- At the loneliest moment of your life, remember your divine Bracer and be encouraged. He says to you, **"I will never leave you nor forsake you....Be strong and very courageous" (Joshua 1:5b, 7a NIV).**

Such a God is worthy of celebration. Celebrate Him; in Jesus' Name. Amen.

Family of God

YOU ARE GOD'S!

Belonging is such an important thing in life that sometimes it determines whether someone is arrogant, proud or humble, happy or depressed, and free or enslaved. Many children have lived with me over the years, who are not my biological kids. Sometimes I understand the level of our attachment from the way they call me: "Uncle" or "Daddy." The appellation is not an indication of differential treatment I have given them but rather an indication of how much attachment they feel or want with me. I remember two siblings who have lived with me. To one I am "Uncle" and to the other I am "Daddy." You belong to God but what you get from Him depends on how you decide to relate with Him, close or distant.

David starts Psalm 24 with a strong declaration, **"The earth is the Lord's, and everything in it, the world, and all who live in it; for he founded it on the seas and established it on the waters" (Psalms 24:1-2 NIV)**. That is a strong declaration. His explanation of this ownership is that God founded the earth and God made you. But this is a strong introduction because David continues in the Psalm to explain why not everyone gets the same attention from God. Those who would receive attention and a blessing from God are:

- Those with clean hands.
- Those who seek Him.
- Those who open their hearts for God to come in.

"They will receive blessing from the Lord and vindication from God their Savior" (Psalms 24:5 NIV). Beloved, God made you. God cares about you. God wants the best for you and desires to dish it out for you. Accept that God is your Daddy, your "Abba Father!" Both in prayer and in the reading of His word, seek His guidance in all you do and let Him lead you to the best.

You belong to your Father God; the earth, and its fullness belong to Him. That means that out of the abundance on earth God will meet your need. May that be your portion in Jesus' Name. You do not only belong to God. He is mindful of you and cares enough about you to meet you at your very point of need. Accept Him that way and be blessed, in Jesus' Name.

CHRISTIAN: GOD IS CELEBRATING YOU!

What does the world celebrate? Success, accomplishments, promotions, acquisitions and victories are a few. I can still see the convoy at Mom's funeral. I lost count of the number of cars involved. It was grandiose, fulfilling and almost looked like it was a great thing to die. Of course, she was not part of the celebration, and it was more for us than for others. However, it was a huge celebration. Is that not common? Every day we read about others being celebrated, exalted and hailed. You probably have wondered when your own celebration will be. You even complain or silently wonder to yourself and maybe even to God that if you do not have children who will celebrate you when you die.

Today God wants you to know that by virtue of belonging to Him, you're important and worth celebrating in God's heart. Imagine that, **"... there will be more rejoicing in heaven over one sinner who repents than over ninety-nine righteous persons who do not need to repent" (Luke 15:7 NIV).** If the inhabitants of heaven celebrated you so much when you gave your life to Christ, what happens when you give your heart to serving Him, living for Him and honoring His Name? God celebrates it greatly.

Job was greatly honored but he surely did not know it because God did not tell him. Rather, God spoke to Satan about His most honored servant, Job.

"One day the angels came to present themselves before the Lord, and Satan also came with them. Then the Lord said to Satan, 'Have you considered my servant Job? There is no one on earth like him; he is blameless and upright, a man who fears God and shuns evil'" (Job 1:6, 8 NIV).

God was happy with Job and He was proud of Job's life.

Dear child of God, if you are saved and as long as you do well in your life with Christ, God is celebrating you. Whether you do what the earth can consider worth celebrating or not, know that God is celebrating you. That is the reason to celebrate. You are not important for your accomplishments; you are important for who you are as a child of God. Therefore, be happy, not for your achievements in life but for your status as a child of God. Live your life in joy and fulfillment because the Lord your God is proud of you and celebrates you, in Jesus' Name.

Day 9   *Family of God*

CAN GOD USE YOU TO HELP?

I would have missed school had God not provided someone who helped me to get an exit visa and reschedule my flight without any charges. In fact, I was able to make that particular trip because another friend paid for my ticket to come home. I could not afford it with the financial assistance I received as a student. I needed the trip home for psychological reasons, and I had an encounter with God during that trip that changed my whole life story. The person who paid for my ticket to come could not even imagine that it was an investment that would have eternal influence. Never play down what God might want to use you to do for someone, no matter how small it might be!

Think about it: for forty days, the Philistines were troubling Israel. Goliath would make noise and threaten them. Everyone, including the soldiers, would run off. All Israel was shaking with fear and no one tried to face Goliath nor come up with a military strategy for conquering him. Forty days! Then, a young shepherd boy showed up. First, he had to face the rejection of his own brothers and then convince the king to let him face Goliath. In the end David brought Goliath down and cut off his head,

"Then the men of Israel and Judah surged forward with a shout and pursued the Philistines to the

entrance of Gath and to the gates of Ekron. Their dead were strewn along the Shaaraim road to Gath and Ekron. When the Israelites returned from chasing the Philistines, they plundered their camp" (1 Samuel 17:52-53 NIV).

Please note these realities:
David had no military experience, but he had other experiences which gave him courage. God can use you out of your own field of expertise. You just need to listen, be sure that He has spoken to you, then let Him use you.

- David was not coming to the war zone to fight. He came to give food to his brothers. God can surprise you and use you where you were not planning to be used. Be open to His guidance.
- David had full courage in his sling, standing against a giant with a javelin (big spear) in his hand, because David trusted God to help him. David's God is the same God you trust, through faith in Jesus Christ.

Beloved in The Lord, as God used David to free a whole nation, he can use you to deliver a whole village or even a nation from whatever particular trouble they may have. Be available for God. Be ready also when God wants to use you for small things that look insignificant so you do not minimize them. A little act, like giving a piece of bread to a hungry person, paying tuition for one year for a child in elementary school, or giving some money to some tired-looking roadside unknown person to pay for a taxi, could have an enormous eternal impact. The man who gave me my first wristwatch around 1980 was in my mind and prayers until he died. Helping someone could place your name in the grace of heaven without you knowing so. God can use you. Let God use you to bless others and you will be blessed, in Jesus' Name.

DO NOT EXPLOIT, EXPLORE!

Why would someone have an opportunity of a lifetime and squander it with the passion of "much now?" Hunger for short-term gain has destroyed many. There is this girl I know whose relatives took her as a daughter after her parents passed away. Her job was simple; take care of the two-room house they lived in, cook, and be ready to take care of the baby when the pregnant mother of the house was delivered. Sadly, she confessed that she would marry a rich person and so did not see the need to bother herself with work. She spent much more of her time basking in the sun than even cleaning the small house. It was so bad that she was sent back to her father's house. She never got to marry a rich man.

What if Hagar had appreciated Sarah for promoting her from slave girl to a co-wife? How beautiful it would have been if she acknowledged with thanksgiving the gift of a baby and praised her mistress for it. There would have been joy in the family for her, the child would have been a delight for Sarah and Abraham would have been a happy father. Instead, **"When she knew she was pregnant, she began to despise her mistress"** (Genesis 16:4 NIV). Her attitude poisoned the whole house and Sarah's inability to contain her led to Sarah contending with Hagar. Interestingly, when the angel saw her running away, he told her: "**'Go back to your mistress and submit to her'**"

(Genesis 16:9 NIV). She had no choice, but she had already distorted the peace and tranquility of the home. She had already diluted the love in that home and worse, she had already invited a curse on her baby, which the Lord declared! Had she explored the possibilities of growth as a loving member of the family, she would have brought joy to it and a great future for herself and a child.

Beloved, sometimes there are second chances. Sometimes those second chances are hard to come by. When God gives you an opportunity to serve, no matter how minimal and how insignificant the opportunity is, serve well and explore the possibility of growth there. Is it not painful and embarrassing that African investors should bring employees from out of the continent because they are looking for honest people? How sad it is that thousands are unemployed because those at the top use the opportunity to exploit the nation of her resources, the company of its capital, or the institution of its running cost, all for selfish reasons.

"Whatever you do, work at it with all your heart, as working for the Lord, not for human masters, since you know that you will receive an inheritance from the Lord as a reward. It is the Lord Christ you are serving. Anyone who does wrong will be repaid for their wrongs, and there is no favoritism" (Colossians 3:23-25 NIV).

God will not only repay for wrongdoing, but He also blesses and will bless for doing it right and open doors for progress. May the Lord grant you the grace to serve faithfully, bless abundantly, and open doors for greater progress, that you may be blessed and be a blessing to many more, in Jesus' Name.

Omnipresent

Day 11 *Omnipresent*

GOD WILL HEAR YOU!

I have a very good friend who cares a lot about me and reaches out from time to time. But it is hard to get to him most of the time when I need him. It takes me a long drive to get to his residence. A couple of times in the past I struggled to get there, only to be turned back at the gate, either because they are having an afternoon rest or because there is no proof of any appointment with him. It can be difficult sometimes to get the attention of people though they care or at least, they do not despise you. God, on the other hand, is always available. He hears!

David was a man of many sorrows throughout his life. While a shepherd of his father's sheep, he had to deal with the attacks of a bear at one time and a lion at another. He killed them each with his hands. Then God called him to the administration of Israel, but it took him about thirteen years of battle with the ruling King Saul before David ascended the throne of Israel. As king, he faced a coup d'état from his son who was finally killed, bringing David tears to the disdain of his soldiers. Later, as king, David's adultery with Bathsheba and killing her husband did not make things any better for him. Amidst all these, he brought Israel to peace on all sides of the nation. He triumphed over all their enemies and could have even built a temple had God not refused him that desire. How did he do this? God always listened to him and strengthened him. That is why he counsels you and me to, **"Look to the Lord and his strength; seek his face always" (1 Chronicles 16:11 NIV).**

Beloved in the Lord, take to heart this counsel from David. In any difficulty, call on God. If it is an urgent need, call on Him. God will always hear you. Sin does separate us from Him and sometimes makes it look as if He is deaf and does not hear. But even with the separation that sin causes, God will hear your cry of repentance for forgiveness. There are no gates and no gatemen to keep you from the presence of God. Reach out to Him. He will hear you for He is always listening. He will respond to you out of His love and care. May the Lord hear you, reach out to you and grant the desires of your heart, in Jesus' Name.

Day 12   *Omnipresent*

GOD IS THERE ALWAYS: FOR YOU!

Have you been in a situation where you depended on someone only to turn around and realize that the person was not there? A friend told me the story of his relative who was looking for greener pastures abroad and hired a company to help with her travel documents. The company gave her the impression that all was well. When she got to the airport in the country, someone would welcome her and give her directions. Well, she got to the airport, and no one was there to welcome her. Neither the person's telephone number she was to see at the airport nor the one the company that sent her was going through anymore. With much assistance from the family back home, she was able to struggle through the painful days to finally find her feet on the ground of that country. What an abandonment! What a struggle!

Sometimes life looks like this lady's story. You come to the earth as a baby brought forth by people who did not ask your opinion before birthing you. Then, at some point you realize that they are not there for you, either because they do not have anything, or they do not care about you. They may have been taken away from you by death. You find yourself stranded in life and wonder what to do and where to go, or who to turn to for help. Life can be challenging!

The good news, friend, is that no one comes to the earth by accident and the one responsible for the birth of all of us is always there to care. The visible human beings, and all those who care for us, are instruments in God's hands. God says: **"Can a mother forget the baby at her breast and have no compassion on the child she has borne? Though she may forget, I will not forget you! See, I have engraved you on the palms of my hands; your walls are ever before me"** (Isaiah 49:15-16 NIV).

The question of a mother having no compassion for the child she has borne is a real one. Yes, babies have been left to die shortly after birth by non-compassionate mothers. We have people saved from the bush, from gutters, and from dustbins, who God rescued to become great people. God values human life. He created the human being in His image.

Beloved of God, if God can rescue those who were totally helpless, God can rescue you who are able to read this devotional. Whatever situation life may hold for you, turn your eyes upon Jesus, and cry out to Him for gracious sustenance. God is able to take care of you completely. Even if you have done some very stupid things and feel guilty and ashamed to look to God, still look up to Him. His grace abounds and is sufficient to forgive and take care of you. As you go through the struggles of life and get to where it is really hard and God is not taking the situation away, remember Paul's experience when he complained to

God and got His reply: **"My grace is all you need. My power works best in weakness"** (**2 Corinthians 12:9a NIV**). If your life is with Jesus, you serve the same God as Paul. In 2022 the children and other dependents of people in my town of residence perished in a landslide. Please pray for their families. They too are God's children. The Lord will take care of them and you, always, in Jesus' Name.

Day 13   *Omnipresent*

THE LORD SHALL COME TO YOUR RESCUE!

Sometimes in life we get into difficulties or even trouble, not because we have done something very wrong but because life in a fallen world is hard. The good news is, God is always there to rescue us. I had come home on holiday from Britain and was about to go back. My luggage was all checked in and I excitedly said goodbye to my family and friends who were with me at the airport. I was at the last security check just before walking to the waiting room when I got a mighty shock. "You must go back. You cannot travel because you do not have an exit visa," I was told. It was a bombshell! My family members and my pleadings to the airport authorities were in vain. I had no idea that I needed an exit visa to leave the country. In my first trip it was not needed, probably because it was the government that prepared all my papers for departure. I went back home, with all my things including the perishable foodstuff that would not survive the wait. Thanks to a great friend, JRN, I was able to reschedule my flight at no cost and traveled a few days later, with an exit visa JRN helped me get the very next day. Though I lost my food, God saw me through.

The Arameans had taken siege of Israel, and the nation was in such bad shape that two women agreed to kill and eat their children. They started with one but the next day the other refused to bring her child for slaughter according to their agreement. That was how bad the nation was. Hunger was at its peak and the nation was on the verge of collapse. Well, the story of the two women reached the king and Prophet Elisha told the king that God was coming to the rescue of the nation. Israel got up the next morning to a mighty victory without having fought,

"For the Lord had caused the Arameans to hear the sound of chariots and horses and a great army, so that they said to one another, "Look, the king of Israel has hired the Hittite and Egyptian kings to attack us!" So they got up and fled in the dusk and abandoned their tents and their horses and donkeys. They left the camp as it was and ran for their lives" (2 Kings 7:6-7 NIV).

Hallelujah! They heard the army of the Lord and fled! Israel was rescued.

Beloved in the Lord, when God gets involved in your life it makes a total difference. There is no situation He cannot handle, no hurdle He cannot get you over, and no trap out of which He cannot rescue you. He is worthy of trust in times of need.

- Are your personal difficulties, problems in the office, or your business becoming stagnated and causing you pain? God will rescue you, in Jesus' Name. Trust Him.
- Is your family or community, village or nation becoming so unbearable, suffering attack from within and without or even from natural forces? Trust God to

come to your rescue. In all situations and at all times, hang on to God, trust Him, pray and have great expectations.

Go forward with confidence because, as Job says in **Job 5:19, NIV, "From six calamities he will rescue you; in seven no harm will touch you,"** in Jesus' Name.

Blessed & Blessing

Day 14 *Blessed & Blessing*

YOU ARE SPECIAL!

Even if no one has ever told you and even if no one has ever treated you as such, you are special. This is because you are you, and God thinks about you as you. I grew up knowing that my father had a thatched three-room house, one of which was a parlor or sitting room which was used more as a store than a living room. Never did we ever sit there for anything. Our "parlor" was our kitchen. It was warm, the factory for our food, our storytelling arena, and small enough to keep us together, bonded, with the bed as Dad's favorite place after a long day of tedious labor in the plantation. In my days of innocence, I slept on the other bed in their bedroom. When I grew up, especially while in high school, I had one of the rooms to myself, unless there was a bed in it on which guests slept when they came to stay overnight. Interestingly, I have never even thought about where the girls stayed in that house. There were six of them though they never were all there at the same time as the younger ones came when the elders left.

As the only boy you can imagine what I went through: favor, love, beating, scolding, sometimes even some jealousy, much teaching (formal and informal) and good discipline. How can I forget having a school uniform at the expense of my sister's school year? How can I forget molding sun-dried blocks, used to add two rooms to make the house the popular L form, with my father? Do I need to forget the joyful burden of transforming that L form house into a later twenty-first-century house with a charitable parlor where even at their old age they could now watch TV and sleep on a more comfortable bed? I was the only male hand that was there to help. How can I forget the hunting expeditions with Dad, just the two of us, or the voice of Mum getting me up in the very wee hours of the morning to go to the rice farm and start work while she prepared the food for our day at the farm? I was always on the farm before 6:00 am. We made it and I got educated! Should I not appreciate God for helping me bury them in joy and celebration after agonizing and fighting with God when He asked me to leave Ndu (close to the village) and come to Yaoundé, because I was afraid that being so far would hinder my care for them up to the days of their grave? *What does being special mean to you,* dear friend?

Being special does not mean receiving all the attention, all the good things, no scolding, no discipline and having many possessions. No! Such behavior "spoils the child" not fixes him or her. The one who loves you as special trains you for life, passes you through training furnaces, channels your character and moods and disciplines you for a disciplined and productive life. Peter could not have imagined that he was special in Jesus' heart, receiving all sorts of treatment as training for leadership. Surely, Peter was glad to answer a question and hear Jesus tell him,

"Blessed are you, Simon son of Jonah, for this was not revealed to you by flesh and blood, but by my Father in heaven. And I tell you that you are Peter, and on this rock I will build my church, and the gates of Hades will not overcome it" (Matthew 16:17-18 NIV).

Jesus encouraged His special servant. But shortly after, while scolding him, Jesus' uttered his worst or most harsh words ever, **"Get behind me, Satan! You are a stumbling block to me; you do not have in mind the concerns of God, but merely human concerns" (Matthew 16:23 NIV).** The same Jesus authorized Satan to go after Peter and sift the pride out of him. Peter could not understand when Jesus told him, **"I have prayed for you, Simon, that your faith may not fail. And when you have turned back, strengthen your brothers (…) I tell you, Peter, before the rooster crows today, you will deny three times that you know me" (Luke 22:32, 34 NIV).** The rebukes and the affirmation, the testing and sifting, the teaching and practice, and the presence of Jesus with Peter when his mother had a fever and Jesus healing her were all acts of love and training. In the absence of Jesus, Peter would shine like one well-formed.

Beloved, you are so special to God that God would not pamper you to be spoilt. He would not shower you with all good things and not discipline you for a better, orderly life.

You have such a place in His heart that God would not fail to give you a smile when you have done good, but again, God will rebuke you through a disturbed conscience, or a physical or emotional pain that calls your attention to Him to get the needed attention from Him. You are so special that God would not fail to be there when troubles haunt you, humanity ignores you, work troubles you, or friends betray you. You are so special to Him that He would not relent giving you the full span of your life and of those who are close to you, but He will not let you live beyond your allotted time.

As you go out today, look in the skies and see the beautiful world God has created to give for your smile and admiration; see the beautiful flowers around and remember that you are more beautiful and precious to the Maker of the universe than all flowers put together. Hear the sound of the wind whose nature and direction you cannot see and remember that even when you do not understand what is going on in your life, the One who makes and directs the wind directs your life to a definite course. Before you go out, look inside you and see the King of the universe, settled *in you*, to guide, protect, love! You are so special that even if all the world left you, *you will never walk alone*. The God of all the earth stands by and walks with you to make your life meaningful, profitable and in His perfect time, comfortable, peaceful, healthy, and blessed. Yes, child of God, you are special, in Jesus' Name.

Day 15   *Blessed & Blessing*

YOUR LORD WILL PROVIDE: HONOR HIM WITH IT

I remember with fun and sadness one of my father's good friends, the fon (chief) of the village of my birth. He just loved my father and that encouraged me to visit him from time to time. Each time I went to his palace, he would not immediately recognize me because of his old age. "Who is it?" he would ask. "Bungansa of Warr Quarter," I would answer. His qualification of me was interesting: "Bungansa of Isaiah Nfor; the Bungansa with the big house?" "Nyarr," I would affirm, as tradition demands, and we would have a good conversation. He never talked to me, no matter how short a time it was without mentioning my village house. I don't know why that particular house interested him, but it did, and I liked the house too. Well, somehow, since that house was built almost twenty years ago, I have never spent up to a month in it and have not entered it for about ten years now. However, I have never spent a night out in the cold except by choice. How strange life can be and how misleading property can be if it takes hold of the heart over and above the more important things of life!

Someone said to me the other day, "I really like investing in people because I can invest in all property and build houses, but I will not take any with me and they may even dilapidate and waste after I am gone. People's lives in whom I invest would never be a waste." I told him that his conviction was profound and meaningful.

Peter was concerned that they had left everything to follow Jesus, wondering how that would benefit them. Jesus told him that they would receive a hundred times more of what they had on this earth, while still here and then, eternal life. But when Peter and the other Apostles went to work and started winning souls, they did not even think of houses, boats, or other businesses, except for what they needed to keep the body sound while doing God's work. God blessed them.

When God called Israel out of Egypt back to the Promised Land He had designated for them, He told them that they would be blessed, but warned them:

"For when you have become full and prosperous and have built fine homes to live in, and when your flocks and herds have become very large and your silver and gold have multiplied along with everything else, be careful! Do not become proud at that time and forget the Lord your God, who rescued you from slavery in the land of Egypt" (Deuteronomy 8:12-14 NLT).

 The Lord kept His word in blessing them and in punishing them when they disobeyed Him.

Beloved in the Lord, may the Lord bless and prosper you greatly. He loves to bless and as you come to Him with the sincerity of your heart, He will provide for you and bless you greatly. But, please, dear friend, when God blesses you, do not think about property and forget about people in need. Do not think about sustenance, saving for the rainy days, and forget the God who provided for you. In the management of the things God has given you and in investing for more, remember that this world is a camp through which we are passing. All of what we acquire here physically will remain here and only your impact will endure with you to eternity.

May the Lord meet you at your point or points of need. May the Lord provide abundantly for you. May the Lord open your eyes to the many human needs around you. May the Lord give you the humility to care and the faith to trust Him to keep providing for you. May the Lord enable you to invest in lives, especially for the Kingdom; then, you will be blessed here and hereafter and be a great blessing to others, in Jesus' Name, Amen.

HATE NO ONE!

This is most difficult, especially since it seems God Himself hates those who do wrong. But does He really hate them? Hate is "intense hostility and aversion; extreme dislike or disgust."[2] An enemy is "one that is antagonistic to another"[3] especially ready to cause harm or injury to the opponent. By encouraging that you hate no one, I mean you should not make anyone your enemy, though you have people who hate you, who are enemies to you.

The Jews expected Jesus to liberate them from the Romans. They were under oppression as colonized people and needed freedom. Jesus, instead focused on their own hearts. A great soldier of the Roman army, the centurion, wanted his servant healed. Jesus offered to come home and heal the paralyzed boy. The centurion asked Jesus to simply say a word, and the boy's injuries would be healed. **"When Jesus heard this, he was amazed and said to those following him, 'Truly I tell you, I have not found anyone in Israel with such great faith'" (Matthew 8:10 NIV).** How could He compare the faith of the Roman with that of the Jews? Jesus goes on to tell the disciples that

---

[2] "Hate." *Merriam-Webster.com Dictionary,* Merriam-Webster, https://www.merriam-webster.com/dictionary/hate. Accessed 22 April, 2025.
[3] "Enemy." *Merriam-Webster.com Dictionary,* Merriam-Webster, https://www.merriam-webster.com/dictionary/enemy. Accessed 22 April, 2025.

people from far off Israel will come and enter the Kingdom of God ahead of them. While you are preoccupied with hating someone, God is blessing the person, and he or she is progressing in life. Do not hate anyone:

- So that you can pray for the person. Jesus tells us, **"...bless those who curse you, pray for those who mistreat you" (Luke 6:28 NIV).** It is easier to hate those who mistreat you than to pray for them. It is more helpful to pray that God should liberate them from the spirit driving their hatred. Then, you can relate well, and they too can enter heaven.
- So that you can feed them when need be. Again, the Bible tells us, **"On the contrary: 'If your enemy is hungry, feed him; if he is thirsty, give him something to drink. In doing this, you will heap burning coals on his head'" (Romans 12:20 NIV).** If you hate anyone who hates you, and you have the opportunity to feed that person, you will be tempted to poison him or her. That will be unchristian.
- So, you can do good to him or her. Again, Jesus teaches, **"But to you who are listening I say: Love your enemies, do good to those who hate you" (Luke 6:27 NIV).** Doing good means doing something positive that can improve the life of the other person, in this case, your enemy. Why should you bother about improving the life of someone whose death can free you? *Because he or she is your enemy, and you are not their enemy!*

Beloved in the Lord, hatred is driven by fear, and enmity is driven by lack of love. Yes, be careful with your enemies, but do not fear them. God has your life in His hands. Do not go looking for your enemies to feed them or do good to them, but when the opportunity arises, do not let it pass unused.

Love covers a multitude of wrongs. Love means seeking the best for others. Love your enemies, pray for them, and leave the part of vengeance to God. Our greatest enemy is not human beings but the devil in them, who takes them captive to do his will. Loving prayers can liberate them and make them friends. God can do all things, including turning your enemies into your friends. He needs your cooperation for that to happen. Though you may be hated, do not hate, and the Lord will bless you and bless many through you, in Jesus' Name.

SEEK HIS BLESSING ALWAYS

One thing for which I remember my mother both happily and tearfully, is her level of generosity which sometimes made us angry as children. We would come from school and have nothing to eat immediately because she had given our food to some passers-by during the day. Waiting in hunger for her to cook again was not always easy. Well, I grew to learn that generosity is a great lifestyle. In my adulthood, I met someone I thought was overdoing it. She would be in serious need, get a little money but prefer to pass it to another needy person. I noticed it twice, thrice, many times. I decided to do more in this area as I realized that this person was always smiling, happy, joyous, and impacting people's lives. Very interestingly, people would ask her questions about her car when she had never even had a bicycle! Paradoxically, I also realize that her needs were provided for in interesting ways. God has just opened for her almost unimaginable opportunities for professional progress. She was a very blessed sister.

Many Christians fast and pray, while others work hard but still struggle with insufficiency. Yet, God blesses and likes to bless His people. So, what might the problem be? The answer may be found in the purpose of God's blessings.

"God is able to bless you abundantly, so that in all things at all times, having all that you need, you will

abound in every good work. As it is written: 'They have freely scattered their gifts to the poor; their righteousness endures forever'" (2 Corinthians 9:8-9 NIV).

A few things stand out in this text, including the purpose of God's blessings - abounding (doing many) good works in all things at all times. Many times, we underline our inability to do good through meeting needs, basing the argument on our not having enough for ourselves. Actually, the enough we do not have is more of our wants (the things that would improve our standard of living) than the basic things that sustain our lives. Our basic needs are often met. I am not unaware of the many Christians and unbelievers alike, who are struggling to live from hand to mouth; but that is also why doing good is necessary; to meet such needs. If you can do good by taking care of the needy, you are meeting the purpose for God's blessings. Beloved, seek God's blessing early and be blessed.

- God is able to bless you. Pray to Him and ask Him to bless the works of your hands and provide for you through other means of His choice.
- God also measures your righteousness in terms of your giving to the needy. Be open-handed, meet needs, in and out of church, as a way of being right with God.

Dear friend, when you abound in good works, being open-handed and meeting needs, God will not only be able to bless you in ways you do not imagine, He will also be willing to do so in a way that you do not expect. Do good and God will bless you. Abound in good works and your hands will be abundantly blessed, in Jesus' Name.

Caring & Comfort

Day 18 *Caring & Comfort*

LEAVE IT ALL TO HIM!

The other day a friend told me of their neighbor who ended up with an amputated leg because he had a small wound and neglected it until it became something quite serious. Sadly, I had watched that happen in my own family. A small wound on the leg became the cause of death because it was minimized and ignored. Our people say, "There is nothing too small." It is amazing how we can trust God and leave things to Him but realize that we still carry some of our burdens with us, either those that are too light or those we think we can take care of ourselves. Small things can indeed destroy and kill!

"Endi" was a very strong member of the prayer band and leader in his church. His pastor was surprised that by the time he was trying to get involved, Endi and his wife's marriage was already at a point of no return. All the time they shared prayer points in the Prayer Band meetings and he talked of all his problems except his marriage and family, yet a worm was eating deep into it and destroying it. In the end, the marriage could not be salvaged. Big issues can be solved as well as they can kill if neglected.

Beloved, God is concerned about *all* things that concern you, big or small. Job had big issues and trusted all into God's hands. But he still debated both with God and his friends. At last, when God made things clear to him, Job confessed, **"I know that you can do all things; no purpose of yours can be thwarted" (Job 42:2 NIV).** Solomon is not just talking about vineyards when he writes, **"Catch for us the foxes, the little foxes that ruin the vineyards, our vineyards that are in bloom" (Song of Songs 2:15 NIV).** He is talking about life; about the little spiritual and physical things that destroy relationships. These should be brought under control before they become too dangerous to handle. They are to be handed to God for assistance.

God is concerned about all things that touch your life, regardless of whether they are little or big things, complicated things or straightforward things. Call on Him, hand them to Him and leave them with Him. He will handle them and give you a result that will bless you and bless others. Let the large or small size of nothing frighten you from praying about it. God's ears are all yours because God's heart is filled with the desire to bless you and bless others through you, in Jesus' Name.

Day 19   *Caring & Comfort*

IT IS NOT ABOUT THEIR STRENGTH OR YOURS!

"Jacob," my classmate was young but quite a macho man. I was young and weak. I cannot remember why we were not very good friends. One afternoon he was bent on beating me. School ended for the day and as usual, we had about an hour to trek home, covering over three kilometers. About twenty minutes into the journey, Jacob started trying to beat me. I was no match for him at all and I knew that. He came at me with a fierce and frightful look. I ran away the fastest I could. He followed me and we went running past the crowd of other students. They did not seem to realize the danger I was in despite my cries. They probably thought we were playing. We got to one point where there were some senior students who were bigger boys. I slowed down a little and Jacob gave me two very sound slaps. I yelled at the top of my voice. The senior students descended on him, and I am not sure how he left that place alive. I walked with them a while before finding my way home. It is not always about the strength of your enemies or yours, but about the help available or not, in your time of need.

David was in constant pain almost throughout his reign. He spent over a decade running for his life away from Saul. Then, he faced stiff troubles from his neighbors. Thank God for the victories. He also faced serious troubles in his own household. His testimony:

"Though I walk in the midst of trouble, you preserve my life. You stretch out your hand against the anger of my foes; with your right hand you save me. The Lord will vindicate me; your love, Lord, endures forever - do not abandon the works of your hands" (Psalm 138:7-8 NIV).

When I read, "... You stretch your hand against the anger of your foes," I could see Jacob's fierce face filled with well-vexed wrath and the hands of those tougher senior students descending on him. Jacob's anger melted and was reshaped into fear. That is what happens with our enemies when God raises His hands against them.

Let me add, however, that those senior students saved me because they knew I was not a troublesome boy. During your troubles, remain faithful, prayerful, loving, and caring. God will guide you and vindicate you, clear your way and save you from their hands. You can never overstate David's confession because it is a deep eternal, unarguable, and unchangeable truth. God's love will endure forever.

If you face spiritual danger to your soul, remember that the Lord who saved you cannot abandon you to Satan to retake. No!

- If your emotions have been bombarded to the point of giving up on life, remember that the Spirit of all comfort dwells in your soul and will never leave you alone. His comfort will release you.

- If you face physical danger to your life, remember that God created you for good works and will keep you to accomplish it.
- If you face threats at work from a boss who hates you, who is too strong and has the power to sack you, remember that the God who gave you the job is still alive to fight for you.
- If you face communal danger, remember that God created this world and determined where each nation (including villages and tribes) should live, and God in His power will keep you where He apportioned for you.

Child of God, life is not guided by the strength or weakness of your enemies, neither is security or insecurity found in your strength or weakness. No! Life is about being right with God, reaching or crying out to Him, and trusting Him to deliver you and set a table before you, in the presence of your enemies, not for your pride but for His glory and their salvation. Your Lord goes with you to keep and save you, in Jesus' Name.

Day 20   Caring & Comfort

HE IS THE LORD OF ALL AGE GROUPS!

I was excited when it was time for spiritual warfare prayer in a church. An elderly person walked up to the stage and led the prayer with passion and energy. I could hardly believe that this energy came from someone seeming physically tired. No! The energy was there, and the praying was lively and very interactive. It came to my mind that sometimes the: "I am old;" "I am tired;" "Let the young people do it;" are only excuses from people who do not realize that there is no age limit for serving the Lord. God is the God of all ages. God Himself is ageless.

David said it clearly that before he was formed in his mother's womb, God knew him. He wrote these words as an elderly man, heading towards the end of his life. God had been with him in the womb and accompanied him through his life. In some parts of the world, some youth feel like they do not need God because they have all that they need. Then, they waste their lives in wild living only to realize at old age that life without Christ has no meaning and no future. In other parts, youth are desperate because they see the years going by, the elderly men and women refusing to grow old, sitting on responsibilities they really cannot discharge, while the young ones roam about seeking for something to do. Are the elderly ones afraid of staying off "undischarged responsibilities" to rest, or are they guilty of their wrongdoings and want to stay so they are not painfully called into account for them?

Beloved in the Lord, whatever your age, walk upright. Do what is right and leave your life in God's hand. His promise is clear, **"Even to your old age and gray hairs I am he, I am he who will sustain you. I have made you and I will carry you; I will sustain you and I will rescue you" (Isaiah 46:4 NIV).** Before you were born, God knew you because He made you and has a plan for you. At your young age, trust Him. He has a future for you and will work it out as you trust Him. Are you elderly? Do not fear. Trust God and live right. Rest and depend on Him. As He took care of you in your young age, so shall He in your old age. The Lord is your strength, life and stay; now and always, in Jesus' Name.

Day 21   *Caring & Comfort*

GOD WILL CARE FOR YOU TO YOUR OLD AGE!

Have you ever wondered how a child is born, becomes an orphan (for various reasons) and without parents, grows up and becomes very responsible and lives to an old age? I was uncertain and unhappy about an elderly man whom I thought could have done better in life. When he told me how his father died when he was in standard three, his only brother was murdered by God knows who, and his mother was not able to raise him up, I then understood his struggles and appreciated him more. I had many smiles and much appreciation when I saw him off to his grave in grey hair and feeble eyes. God had blessed him with some good, successful children and took care of him to his old age and to the grave.

Israel was like an orphan, except that God chose to take her away from her living parents. God called Abraham out of his own land (Ur of the Chaldeans) and led him without much human assistance to an unknown land. Abraham stayed in that land and established a family, but as a stranger. God took his descendants, Jacob and his children, from that land to Egypt where they were welcomed and then became an enslaved people, worse than a colony. No human friends: no nation to come and help them out of Egypt. When God finally took them out as a nation, they could not just step into Canaan where they left as a small family. No nation could join them to fight for the Promised

Land. God fought for them, and they traveled into the Promised Land

In the Promised Land, they disobeyed God and He imposed a sanction on them by sending them on exile to Babylon. How sad and depressed they felt! It was like their life as a nation was vanishing before their very eyes. Again, no nation could help them fight Babylon to get them back home. The colonialism was real and their identity was ebbing away. During that uncertainty about their future as a nation; with hopes dashed on the might of Babylon, Israel's jaw dropped in despair. Then God told them through Prophet Isaiah:

"Listen to Me, you descendants of Jacob, all the remnant of the people of Israel, you whom I have upheld since your birth, and have carried since you were born. Even to your old age and gray hairs I am he, I am he who will sustain you. I have made you and I will carry you; I will sustain you and I will rescue you" (Isaiah 46:3-4 NIV).

Note:

- God remined them of their descendancy.
- God reminded them of how He cared for them from birth.
- God committed Himself to their sustenance, until their old age and grey hair.

How great is the God we serve: He renewed their age and now the young nation of Israel, celebrating over 75 years of existence, is one of the strongest countries in the world. That is God at work!

Child of God, if you have believed in Jesus, you are in a covenant relationship with God:

- If you are young and lonely, do not cry about the uncertainties of your future. You may not have a godfather, but you have God the Father who will walk you through your life to your grey hair.
- If you are struggling, even as a people, with no ally or friends to help you, look up to God. He who brought Israel out of Egypt and back from Babylon without human allies will take you safely away from your oppressors and troubles, renew you and keep you to your old age and grey hair.
- If you are at, or nearing your old age and grey hair, look back and appreciate God for what He has and is doing in your life because it is God, not your wits or wealth that has brought you safely to your old age.

From the warmth of the womb to weaning, through life to the grave, look up to Him who is your Strength, and be assured that as long as He is not done with your assignment on earth; to your old age and grey hair, God will keep you, bless you, sustain you, and make you a blessing to yourself, your family and to others in Jesus' Name.

Day 22   *Caring & Comfort*

YOUR BURDEN BEARER!

It is unfortunate that we live in a world where care, concern, and reaching out for help is not always obvious, not even from our own blood family members. Even more saddening is the fact that we can be exploited by our own family. It was not only Cain and Abel in the Bible. No! I know someone who killed his blood brother to collect forty thousand francs CFA ($80). Interestingly, God did not kill Cain in return. He protected him from being killed. Grace!

You may never know if or when you faced the danger of harm or death, but the Lord has been with you. Celebrate His loving and caring goodness to you. Hagar was running away from her Master, not even sure where she was going, pregnant with Abraham's child, amid Sarah's faithlessness and Hagar's opportunism. How could God care for such a person, an opportunist who became proud and arrogant? God knew all about Hagar's position, but as a burden bearer, He sent an angel to her who told her, **"You are now pregnant and you will give birth to a son. You shall name him Ishmael, for the Lord has heard of your misery" (Genesis 16:11 NIV).** The response from Hagar is a beautiful act of worship. **"She gave this name to the Lord who spoke to her: 'You are the God who sees me, for she said, 'I have now seen the One who sees me'" (Genesis 16:13 NIV).** If Hagar had not gotten into trouble, she would not have experienced God's care. God did not abandon her, and God has not abandoned you.

Are you living a life of great difficulty? Identify one thing the Lord has done for you and even give Him a Name connected to that for which He has done. God, our burden bearer is concerned about you always. Out of the experience of God's goodness, David burst out in song, **"Praise be to the Lord, to God our Savior, who daily bears our burdens. Our God is a God who saves; from the Sovereign Lord comes escape from death" (Psalm 68:19-20 NIV).**

Oh, that you will see God's Hand upon your life and cry out in worship to Him. Bless the Lord and be even more blessed, in Jesus' Name.

Day 23   *Caring & Comfort*

THE GREATEST COMFORT IS IN KNOWING GOD!

In my country, Friday and Saturday are almost certainly the days when tears flow the most because many corpses are removed from the mortuary on Friday and buried on Saturday. It is not always easy to have the right words to say to those who have lost their loved ones. How do you tell someone whose wife has died after less than ten years of marriage, leaving a little child for him to manage, that it is well, and he should stop crying? How do you tell parents who have lost their child at his or her prime, that they should not cry because God knows what He is doing? Comforting is hard.

God understands what pain is. When Jesus lost His friend Lazarus, it was painful. He saw Lazarus' sister and the Jews who were there weeping, and He was touched. **"Jesus wept." (John 11:35 NIV).** Paul tells us that there are times when we do not have the words with which to express our deepest pain. At such times of our greatest weakness, we are told, **"In the same way, the Spirit helps us in our weakness. We do not know what we ought to pray for, but the Spirit himself intercedes for us through wordless groans" (Romans 8:26 NIV).** It is good to have a God who is concerned and knows our pain so much He comforts us in our time of deepest need. Again, the assurance that death is not the end but a transition in life, is a reason to be comforted when one loses a loved one.

Tears do not come only with death. Failing an examination, waiting for interventions in vain, having a crisis at work, or losing something of great value may also make one cry. In all these, God is the greatest Comfort.

- He gives assurance at the time of pain, that all will be well. After all, life is in His hands, and nothing happens out of His control. To be reminded of His being in control is comforting.
- He accompanies the concerned in finding the solution, giving comfort.

Beloved, we live in such a world of pain, it is not good for you to be without God at the center of your life. Accept that you are a sinner. Believe that Christ died for you. Confess your sins, repent from them and ask Jesus to take personal control of your heart and of your life. Then, walk each day according to God's word. You will not only have eternal life, but you will be comforted. Whatever is causing you tears now, if you are not a Christian, let Jesus take over the control of your life for your comfort and for your best. If you already know Him, remember the words of Jesus, **"I have told you these things, so that in me you may have peace. In this world you will have trouble. But take heart! I have overcome the world" (John 16:33 NIV).** Hold on to Him and be comforted and have your peace. It is and shall be well, in Jesus' Name. Shalom, Shalom.

Purpose & Plans

Day 24   *Purpose & Plans*

NOTHING IS NEW TO GOD

Have you ever been in a situation where you wonder if God even knows what is going on, and just wonder where your life or the situation for which you are concerned is going? When I got into the town where I started my pastoral ministry after training, I met a young man who took quite good care of my hair. He was handsome and smart, but I could never imagine what the future held for him. One day, I realized he went to high school, and before long, he sat in my class in the seminary to study. More recently, I watched him preside at the graduation ceremony of master's degree students who have sat at his feet for four years. Just hearing the student representative talk, one could hardly doubt the quality of training they have had. Their heads and hearts have been formed for great work. As I watched the associate professor, my mind went back approximately twenty years, and I thought, "God, you knew all this before then and worked it out: thank you, Lord."

Just imagine Abraham looking down from heaven now and seeing how much Christianity is making a difference in people's lives. He thinks of how he left his home in Ur of the Chaldeans when God just called him (God alone knows how long ago). He remembers experiences such as raising his hand to slay his son Isaac, and God stopping it mid-air to instead provide a ram. He can only look at God in humility and pride and say, "Thank you, Lord!"

Beloved in the Lord:

- When good things happen in your life, do not forget that God is working out what He planned many years ago. Be like Prophet Isaiah who saw God at work in Israel and proclaimed, **"Lord, you are my God; I will exalt you and praise your name, for in perfect faithfulness you have done wonderful things, things planned long ago" (Isaiah 25:1 NIV).** Underline the words, "things planned long ago." God's knowledge is not progressive; it is total, from the beginning of all things until when all shall end.
- When you are struggling with situations and not sure where it is all going, look up to Him and know that He has things planned out for you. The outcome of your life will not be a surprise to Him. It will be the outcome of His work in your life for years past.
- When your village, city or nation is going through stress and difficulties and it even looks like it will be wiped out, remember that God is still in charge. Those hard times are part of His working things out to glorify Himself and give a future and life to your village, community or nation.

Nothing is new to God, not just because He knows all things before they come to pass, but also because He is in charge. Life, at all levels and at all times is in His hand. Let no problem, difficulty or great blessing surprise you. Look up to God in each case and exalt Him because your life will be in His hands, in Jesus' Name.

Day 25   *Purpose & Plans*

DIFFERENT PROBLEMS: SAME GOD!

God, the creator of heaven and of all humanity, is the same God who is concerned and handles the problems of the rich and the poor, the knowledgeable and the ignorant. Together with some friends, we were discussing high school life. Even in the village where some of us schooled, there were children of a little more well-to-do people. But the difference between them and the children of the needy did not show so much. My friends who schooled in cities had much more visible differences. Some of them described how they came to school in the rain, but their friends were escorted into the classrooms from beautiful cars under umbrellas. Some went to school bare-footed while their classmates came fully dressed in no ordinary shoes. As we sat talking with everyone now in the professional world, you could no longer distinguish between children of the poor and those of the rich. They all wrote the same exams, went through the same training in various fields and now face the same challenges as adults. Reality treats all alike.

Two stories are recorded back-to-back in 2 Kings chapter four. First, a widow is indebted, and the creditor would not let her and her two children rest. She cried out to prophet Elisha; God heard her and solved her problem miraculously. The second problem is with a well-to-do woman who had no child. Elisha came to her aid.

"'About this time next year,' Elisha said, 'you will hold a son in your arms.' 'No, my Lord!' she objected. 'Please, man of God, don't mislead your servant!' But the woman became pregnant, and the next year about that same time, she gave birth to a son, just as Elisha had told her" (2 Kings 4:16-17 NIV).

While the former had children and lacked money, the latter had money and lacked children. The same God solved their problems.

Beloved in the Lord,

- Whoever you are and whatever you have, humble yourself before God. No matter what comfort you have, you will face difficulties in life that wealth, influence, and connectedness cannot solve. God alone will know best how to solve them.
- Never feel you are too big to relate with some people. You never know where God is taking you and who you will need in the years ahead of you.
- Respect and honor all those around you. We live in the same world, face different but similar problems, and need different but similar solutions. When you stand in line at the supermarket, pay for the groceries of that person in front of you who is struggling and looks neglected.
- Also, as you live daily, remember that all of us will stand before the same judgment throne to be judged and charged or acquitted by the same God.

- More graciously, the one thing that unites Christians should be at the heart of all our relationships: Jesus Christ.

"... for all of you who were baptized into Christ have clothed yourselves with Christ. There is neither Jew nor Gentile, neither slave nor free, nor is there male and female, for you are all one in Christ Jesus" (Galatians 3:27-28 NIV).

In Christ alone is our hope, our love, our life, our stay, our future and our eternity. May that fact guide your life for in it is hidden your greatest treasure. In Christ, may we all be blessed and bless others, in Jesus' Name.

Day 26 *Purpose & Plans*

THE WAY TO GREATNESS IS DEATH!

The sentiment that death and greatness are related did not make sense to me immediately but did get me thinking. Talking about Jesus, the Bible says:

"And being found in appearance as a man, he humbled himself by becoming obedient to death - even death on a cross! Therefore God exalted him to the highest place and gave him the name that is above every name" (Philippians 2:8-9 NIV).

Jesus was exalted to a Name above all other names because He was obedient to death. Yes! You die, then you live to be great!

I read the story of an American rich man who traveled mostly by public transport and used his money to do a lot of charity work. He laid aside his comfort for other people. One of the wealthiest people I know in my own country makes himself available for children's birthdays and knows the names of almost all his grandchildren and the children in his extended family. He plays with the youth and dines with the great. He is seen with the masses and provides for them when there is need. He advocates well for the oppressed. He is great among the young when he shows up and enjoys children, giving them much honor. At the end of the day, he is great among all.

Pride and greatness can go together temporarily, leading to a fall. Nebuchadnezzar experienced it. His true greatness came when he confessed there was a God in the universe greater than himself. He was ready to die to himself and to that God. Nelson Mandela was ready to die when he took up guns against the white South African autocrats. He was willing to endure suffering and remain in a cell for almost three decades, refusing all forms of negotiations. These could probably have given him much money and make him great in wealth, but death was better for him. My most memorable picture of Mandela is as a president in a short sleeve shirt, a sign of his humility.

Africa is suffering so much because there are few, if any political leaders who are ready to lay down their comfort, their wealth, their pride, indeed their lives; for the good, liberty and progress of their people. Many churches suffer because some pastors see the pulpit as a farm. They see Christians with their families as the crops they harvest for their wealth and comfort. Universities are suffering because professors are not ready to sacrifice to help the students grow. Many of them transfer their professions into politics and make such a dirty game out of it they speak like people who have lost their senses, talking like uneducated people. This is all to defend positions and for the possibility of embezzling funds, leaving their students stranded and the people suffering.

Beloved, unless you are ready to die to self, you are not ready to be great. Yes, you can occupy great positions in society and be hailed for that but still end up as just one of those who were there. True greatness comes from dying to self and living for God and others. You can say like Paul,

"What is more, I consider everything a loss because of the surpassing worth of knowing Christ Jesus my Lord, for whose sake I have lost all things. I consider them garbage, that I may gain Christ" (Philippians 3:8 NIV).

Do that! Lay aside all things pertaining to self, for God and for people; and you will be on the highway to greatness; blessed and blessing others, in Jesus' Name.

Day 27   *Purpose & Plans*

WHAT DO YOU HAVE: VISION OR FANTASY?

Thinking about the future is an important part of life. Perceptions can make or mar someone's walk into the future. There was a young lady who lived with us and all she talked about was how she would marry a rich man. As a result, she did nothing in the house although she came to live with us to serve us. Marrying a rich man was not a vision, it was a fantasy. On the other hand, there was a group of children who were about one class apart who went to school about the same time. They all decided that they would be telecommunication engineers. They started their primary school around the time cell phones were introduced in Cameroon which might have influenced their vision formation. All of them ended up in the IT field and one actually had a first degree in telecommunication engineering, before switching to electrical engineering for post-graduate work. Vision and fantasy are different. You need a vision, not a fantasy.

A vision and a fantasy are both what you see about the future. They are images you build in your mind about the future and hope to arrive at that point which get those images to come to pass. But they are different:

A vision is a state of reality you see about the future which you can make come to pass. No matter how remote the possibility it is for you to make it happen, there is at least that possibility. When the children decided to become engineers, they insisted they would study science subjects in high school. They all had very good grades in physics and mathematics. A vision is more than just a wish; it is a desire you work to accomplish, trusting God for His grace and guidance for you to accomplish it.

A vision can also be a clear revelation from God that comes through a dream, a thought, or a trance. Joseph had a dream-vision that he would lead the family and they would all bow before him. He could not imagine himself becoming a politician, let alone a prime minister. Israel was not even a nation. In fact, it was not even a village where he could be made chief, so his family members would bow to him! But God who gave the vision made it to come to pass. Though it was not clear how it would come about, the brothers and his father believed its possibility, and his brothers decided to kill him for it. That started God's route for Joseph to become a man to who the family would bow. A vision is followed by action or circumstantial happenings (of which you play a part) to make it come to pass.

A fantasy is a thought or desire about the future, but of which there is nothing you can do to make it come to pass. It is: "The power or process of creating especially unrealistic or improbable mental images in response to psychological need."[4] Fantasies are unrealistic. A village girl, who has no connection with any rich family and who has no education, deciding she will marry a rich person, is a fantasy. She has no way of making it happen and cannot say that it is a revelation from God. For her to work for it to come to pass, she should become self-promoting, carrying herself into the realm of the rich. But she has no means at all! So, she becomes lazy because of it and ends up distracted in life. Solomon said, **"Those who work their land will have abundant food, but those who chase fantasies will have their fill of poverty. A faithful person will be richly blessed, but one eager to get rich will not go unpunished"** (Proverbs 28:19-20 NIV).

Beloved in the Lord, as you think about the future, ask God for a vision. Those who make a difference in their lives and in the lives of others are people led by a vision. In whatever you do, ask God what He has in mind for you for the years ahead and ask Him to lead you to it. Be focused and work for it. Do not let your mind build fantasies, castles in the sand, void of your ability to accomplish or impact others. Most fantasies have to do with the desire to become rich, without an appropriate means of getting there. Even if you get there, you could be self-destroyed because you had no objective to accomplish with the wealth. A vision is a life-

---

[4] "Fantasy." *Merriam-Webster.com Dictionary,* Merriam-Webster, https://www.merriam-webster.com/dictionary/fantasy. Accessed 22 April, 2025.

driver. It leads to great accomplishment and great influence. It creates a focused life that refuses distractions. Ask God for it, get it and run with it into a blessed future that will bless many others, in Jesus' Name.

God's Beauty

Day 28 — God's Beauty

MAY THE LORD GROW AND GLOW YOUR HEART!

I entered the class for the first time for that academic year and saw a woman seated in it. At first, I was startled at her beauty. "What kind of fairness is this that makes someone look so artificial? Has she worked on her skin and rubbed something on it or is this natural?" I pondered. Of course, it was a very quick thought as I would not let it stay there and distract me from the class. During the class, I realized that she was a woman of very high social standing but was extremely simple, approachable, and kind. I was even more surprised after class when she followed me to the car and asked softly and smiling, "Sir, what kind of product do you use that makes you so middle-sized? I want to lose weight. Can you share your secret with me?" That started a relationship that took me to their very simple but posh home.

I sat at table with the couple only to be told, "Sir, enjoy your meal. We are on our twenty-one day fast." The stories of their upbringing, education, meeting, marrying, professional progress, and spiritual journeying were a clear indication of nobility, not of social standing but the nobility of the heart. By the way, I could not tell if he was more handsome than she was beautiful. Their hearts glowed with love for God and had a deep appreciation of the Lord's enabling them to dodge the satanic arrows often directed at the upper class. They remain humble and loving people. Ah! When you allow God to touch your heart, He gives you such charm that the nations tremble when you pass by.

The secret to this success was her mother. She kept her directed, guided and protected from all the young guys that rallied around her beauty. She planted both fear and a fight against error in her heart. Second, the patience, endurance, and quiet resilience of the man who was neither anxious nor ready to give up but wait for her heart and mind to develop over the years and not being afraid that he might lose her, was greatly aided by his father who knew the story early and loved and protected her for his son. You see, there is something about the beauty of the heart. It does not shout, but its results do. The beauty of the heart protects the beauty of the outer skin and keeps it from the danger of intruding nectar suckers. The beauty of the heart finds it's sweetest expression in the Biblical woman, a mother.

"She speaks with wisdom, and faithful instruction is on her tongue. She watches over the affairs of her household and does not eat the bread of idleness. Her children arise and call her blessed; her husband also, and he praises her" (Proverbs 31:26-28 NIV).

The beautiful heart invests in the home and harvests the result in the success and appreciation of the children. The author of the poem does not forget to make a comparison with the outer beauty. **"Charm is deceptive, and beauty is fleeting; but a woman who fears the Lord is to be praised. Honor her for all that her hands have done, and let her works bring her praise at the city gate" (Proverbs 31:30-31 NIV).**

Dear child of God: appreciate the beauty or handsomeness God has given you and do not allow anyone to convince you that you are not beautiful or handsome. They did not make you what you are, God did. You are beautiful or handsome in His sight.

- Never be tempted to use charm to attract the one for whom you cannot patiently wait. Charm is deceptive and expires. When it does, the effect is a dangerous snare on the face of the one you charmed; such a snare that you cannot clear off easily.
- Develop your heart and invest in his or her heart. In so doing, you will be making a worthwhile, lifelong, joy-yielding, family building, and God-glorifying investment.

"Above all else, guard your heart, for everything you do flows from it" (Proverbs 4:23 NIV). May the Lord guide you to guard over your heart, and to help those in your circle of influence to guard over their hearts. That is a highway to protracted blessing for you and others. May that be your portion, in Jesus' Name.

Day 29 — God's Beauty

WHAT GOD, WHAT ME!

It is over thirty-two years now, but I can still hear us in one voice, without error in notes or pitch, raising our hearts in worship to the Lord, in the fifteen-hundred-man choir. It had taken us six months to build this choir that would last just a week, but would preach and worship in song, alongside evangelist Billy Graham. When I think of that experience and remember the awesomeness of the choir and the wonder of the worship it raised, I cannot even imagine what worship in heaven is like. Think about all the wonderful musicians who have passed through this earth, including David and Handel. Think about all the beautiful voices you have heard that have made your hair sometimes stand on end in wonder. Think about the voices of thousands and tens of thousands upon tens of thousands of angels, all in one voice and song! What a choir, what a worship! What are they singing? **"The heavens declare the glory of God; the skies proclaim the work of his hands" (Psalm 19:1 NIV)**

Psalm 19:1 puts heaven and the skies together in its beautiful message. While the heavens (all in heaven) declare the glory of God; the skies, the physical expression of God's beauty, proclaim the works of God's hand. Lift up your eyes to the skies and look at the clouds, the sunshine, and its colors. Then, go online and look at the images of various parts of the world including the Mandara mountains of Cameroon, the Grand Canyon in the USA and the Swiss ski mountains! Look at the images coming to us from space, other planets and galaxies through NASA and other space explorers! To think that One mind made all these breathtaking images and is telling of the greatness of God.

The beauty of the physical world tells that you are fearfully and wonderfully made. If God can put such great beauty in what is here now and gone tomorrow, how much more effort has He put in making you and me in His image? When someone makes you think you are not beautiful or handsome, or when someone tells you that you are not great simply because you do not have a great job or occupy a wonderful position in society, tell them there is something called intrinsic value and beauty in each person of God's creation. That fact alone makes everyone He has made great. As the Psalmist says, I am fearfully and wonderfully made! Should you not be proud and worship God for that? Sin has marred but not destroyed the image of God in the human being. What a God! What a me! What a you!

Beloved, the great choir in heaven declaring the glory of God has just one theme for all their songs. It is glory to God for the Lamb that was slain. In our choir in Aberdeen, over thirty years ago, the most serious song we sang, which I can see Steve Barrows leading, conducting and passionately getting us to sing each evening was, "Just as I am without one plea, but that Thy blood was shed for me and that Thou bids me come to Thee, Oh Lamb of God I come, I come." The theme is the same: the Lamb, Jesus, gave His life that we might live. There is nothing more important than that in all creation. Nothing! Nothing!

Dear friend, loved of God, if something this important preoccupies all of heaven, it should be vitally important to you too. If Jesus has not yet made a salvation difference in your life, I pray you open up to His saving grace. If He has, may you make soul-winning a priority in your life, while assuring yourself that the intrinsic value of your greatness is reflected in the greatness of the Mind that created you. Ah! You are so important to God! You are so blessed to be alive and enjoy the joy of the Lord as a saved one. Be a great blessing and put a song of salvation into someone's life. May it be a song and smile in heaven, in Jesus' Name.

Day 30 God's Beauty

ENJOY THE BEAUTY OF GOD

My friend lives by the city garden called the Rose Garden. This is their best time of the year as flowers bud and bloom. It is truly beautiful to gaze at the garden and enjoy the roses, the daffodils and many other beautiful flowers, not even in their backyard but just by their window. I could imagine her smiling when she wrote to me the other day, including pictures, "Rose Garden...the daffodils in my yard are just beginning to bud. They should be pretty...." You see, not only the eyes but also the heart and the mind like beauty. When I had a small garden at the door to our house, I realized that people smiled when they came home, even when they were coming with a difficulty that was enough to take the smile away before we started conversing.

But one thing I have also realized is that there is a level of pain that causes the beauty appealing to the physical eyes to lose its meaning. Someone stricken by the death of a loved one, for example, does not have the mind to see even the most beautiful flower or the most beautiful or handsome person standing there. For such a person there is another "beauty" that is attractive, healing, sustaining, and strengthening. It is the beauty of the Lord. David was a man of pain, of battles, and of war. But his mind was constantly on the temple. He said:

"Though an army besiege me, my heart will not fear; though war break out against me, even then I will be confident. One thing I ask from the Lord, this only do I seek: that I may dwell in the house of the Lord all the days of my life, to gaze on the beauty of the Lord and to seek him in his temple" (Psalm 27:3-4 NIV).

The temple was beautifully built long after David lived. He could not, therefore, be talking about the beauty of the temple. God is not visible to human physical eyes for David to have seen. What then did he mean by the beauty of the Lord? While we enjoy the physical appearance as beautiful, there is a beauty produced by character or personality. The person who is loving, kind, caring, humble, gentle, and always ready to intervene and help is a "beautiful" person. That is God. Of course, God would not smile at sin, but He would forgive enough to make the repentant sinner smile and be glorified. Dwelling in the house of the Lord is being conscious of the perpetual, unfailing presence of God. Gazing on the beauty of the Lord means depending, trusting, and being fully satisfied with the goodness and love of God at all times. Seeking God in His temple means desiring to know His will and living by it.

Dear friend, remember that God is continually present with you to guide and keep you on the safe path. May the beauty, the goodness and loving heart of God fill you with assurance that in whatever situation, it will be well with you, no matter how many days or how long you experience the difficulties of life. The Lord will be there for you. After all, **"The steadfast love of the Lord never ceases; his mercies never come to an end; they are new every morning; great is thy faithfulness" (Lamentations 3:22-23 RSV.)** May the beauty of the Lord make each of your days most beautiful, most blessed and most blessing, in Jesus' Name.

Creator & Creation

CELEBRATE THE CREATOR OF NATURE

One of the things I miss from home, and particularly from my childhood years, is the enjoyment of the clear night sky when the moon is full and shining brightly. When bush lamps and traditional candle lamps were our source of reading light, we used to say that one could read with the moonlight, which we actually tried sometimes when things were really hard. More exciting though, was when we moved up and down from Center to Nshwi and Ngashung all in Mbawrong, Njirong village (Northwest, Cameroon) during the rice harvest season. The day was extremely hot and the moon enabled us to enjoy the cold of the night, just moving around the village. In the residential part of our village at that time, we practiced our Christmas plays and songs best in the moon-lit night; otherwise, we played many children's games. Somehow, the coming of electrical light has taken away such joyful activities from the village because people are busy working even at night.

The God who created the natural environment truly loves humanity. Humankind lives out of the soil. The mountains and the hills feed the eyes and the emotions. The skies give humanity its needed rain and heat, dull weather and sunshine, all in the right season. The next time you pick or buy flowers to express love for someone or when you walk out of your door to your beautiful garden (planted or natural), remember that those beautiful flowers are not just the result of your floriculture, they are a manifestation of the Creator and Sustainer of the universe who gave nature to mankind. Our Creator keeps it for us with all its designs and variations. The writer of Genesis puts a cap on the creation story when he says: **"Thus the heavens and the earth were completed in all their vast array" (Genesis 2:1 NIV).** There is nothing in all creation that God did not make, no matter how little or big.

God did not make nature to be worshipped and does not dwell in nature. He cannot be reduced to living in a cave, a mountain, a river or wherever in nature. No! He is above nature. **"The Lord is exalted over all the nations, his glory above the heavens. Who is like the Lord our God, The One who sits enthroned on high, who stoops down to look on the heavens and the earth?" (Psalm 113:4-6 NIV).** God stoops down to look at the heavens that are higher than the earth. And, He will keep nature to feed your stomach and your eyes for as long as time lasts. **"He is The Maker of heaven and earth, the sea, and everything in them - he remains faithful forever" (Psalm 146:6 NIV).** The Creator and Sustainer is the God, Father of our Lord Jesus Christ. Celebrate Him, worship Him and let Him bless and keep you here and into eternity, in Jesus' Name.

Day 32 *Creator & Creation*

WORSHIP THE GOD OF BEAUTY!

It is amazing how the world celebrates beauty. Many love flowers, beautiful landscapes, and even the beauty of humanity. Apart from possibly Nigerian movies, hardly would one watch any movie or advertisement bearing someone who is not very beautiful or handsome. Many people, especially but not only women, spend huge sums of money to find or maintain their beautiful bodies. While a few people have given their lives to God because of their wonder and acknowledgment of the beautiful world around them, many just ignore the original source of every beauty, God.

Sometimes I open sites on the Internet that deal with nature, just to view the beauty of the natural environment. David might have been standing outside with his eyes lifted to the skies when he said to God: **"When I consider your heavens, the work of your fingers, the moon and the stars, which you have set in place, what is mankind that you are mindful of them, human beings that you care for them" (Psalm 8:3-4 NIV).** He was not asking a question that required God's answer. He was just expressing awe, wonder, and amazement at what God has created and the place He has given to humanity within that creation. God must have great love for humanity and for pleasure. He gives us an environment full of things that are beautiful enough to amaze us and make the saddened soul smile. Ah, the God of beauty!

The coming of sin into the world brought trouble upon the beautiful world God created. I cannot even imagine the beauty of the Garden of Eden. It would not have fit the description of a "World's Wonder" because I suspect it was too breathtaking to be described. But here we are, with thorns and thistles characterizing our world today. Even when God gives beauty around us, we misuse it, ignore it, abuse it, and worst of all, worship it. The Israelites even attempted to use the jewelry that God had the Egyptians give them when they were leaving Egypt for idol worship. When Israel got to the desert and Moses went to receive the Ten Commandments, **"They took pride in their beautiful jewelry and used it to make their detestable idols. They made it into vile images" (Ezekiel 7:20a NIV)**. How sad! Yet, in His love and in line with His Being and character as the God of beauty, **"He has made everything beautiful in its time" (Ecclesiastes 3:11a NIV)**. Even death is made beautiful when the dead believed in Christ; and we can look forward to the beauty of the resurrected body. The God of beauty makes beauty out of ashes. He is to be worshiped.

Just step out of your room today or look at the horizon out of your window; when you see the beautiful skies, the setting sun, the beauty of the dark clouds that bring forth rain; when you see the beauty displayed in your garden, the flowers and the grace glittering in the sun, worship the God of beauty. Above all, remember that there is a beauty that God truly appreciates, and you can give it to Him. **"How beautiful on the mountains are the feet of those who bring good news, who proclaim peace, who bring good tidings, who proclaim salvation, who say to Zion, 'Your God reigns" (Isaiah 52:7 NIV).** Make your feet be beautiful beloved, and be a blessing to humanity; give glory and pleasure to God, and be blessed, in Jesus' Name.

Day 33   *Creator & Creation*

HUMAN LIFE IS WORTHY!

I was just over ten years old when I heard, for the first time that someone had died, and her life would be celebrated for over a week. It was the Mayah (the Female Chief) of our village. I was excited. The first day I was there enjoying a lot of dances and traditional displays. There was much singing and dancing, and eating and drinking. To my great shock, my father would not allow me to go in the days that followed. While everyone was rejoicing, he was visibly depressed. His daughter had been crowned the successor to the one who died (got missing, as we put it in our tradition) and that did not please him. It would take me many years to understand that he had reasons to cry. He knew the kind of responsibilities that were conferred on his daughter and what it would take for him to help her succeed. While life can be celebrated for simple existence, the worthiness of life increases greatly when the person lives responsibly and impacts people influentially.

For a month we celebrated the life of a woman who lived 102 years, Mama Miriam Labu Awudu. As I watched groups upon groups come and go, expressing great joy, in song, dance, and food and drink at her son's residence and as I watched over a thousand people congregate in Yaoundé to praise God for her and celebrate her legacy, I could not help noting that I had hardly seen such a celebration of a life. Yes, I have seen lives celebrated for weeks, not because the person had done great things, but because the person was either a traditional ruler or a politician whose funeral was itself a political statement, with much partisan undertones. Mama Labu was a quiet woman who was being celebrated for her influence, impact and love expressed directly and through her son whose love and social impact was without measure.

The human being is worthy, important, and valuable. David was right to cry out in wonder to God,

"When I consider your heavens, the work of your fingers, the moon and the stars, which you have set in place, what is mankind that you are mindful of them, human beings that you care for them? You have made them a little lower than the angels and crowned them with glory and honor." (Psalm 8:3-5, NIV).

Dear friend in the Lord, as you look at yourself as a human being:

- Thank God for just the mere fact of your existence; you are worthy. God has made you so, and no one can change it. Let no one and nothing make you feel worthless. You are important in the eyes of God.
- Do not fail to appreciate the God who created the universe and created and made you so worthy within it; you are more important than all the physical beauty you see in the skies above.

- Live a life of impact and influence in line with how much God has blessed you. Let no one come to you and not be blessed. Where you have an opportunity to go and bless, do not wait for an invitation. Blessing is celebrating both the God who provides for you and the worthiness of the life you bless.
- Never have a good reason to despise a life, ignore a life, maltreat a life, or carelessly take away a life. In doing so, you will be putting yourself at loggerheads with the God who created the life. Instead, look for ways to take away the factor that is attacking you to despise, maltreat, ignore or take away the life. Whether the cause is poverty, irresponsibility, failure, misbehavior, or rebellion, you will be a hero, at least in God's eyes and in the eyes of the individual, if you even painfully, restore such a life to worth, dignity and honor.

Live to bless others and impact them. Then, you will be celebrated, not for your financial riches nor your position, but for your influence, which added worth to the worth of human beings around you as you had their need met. That is a highway to being blessed. Take it and be blessed and be a blessing, in Jesus' Name.

Deliverance & Care

Day 34   *Deliverance & Care*

YOUR GOD WILL ARISE!

It is hard to struggle in the presence of the One who you know has the answers to your troubles. A brother's complaints to me were realistic and almost very convincing. "Muh" lived with his uncle who sponsored him through a very good professional school. He graduated with a good grade. Unfortunately, he did not have a job and was angry that his uncle was not caring enough for him to get a job for him. He forgot all the good things the uncle had done for him including the training he had received at the uncle's expense.

God brought Israel from Egypt and took good care of them. Yet, they were stubborn, which made God quite unhappy. When God sent them into exile, it was like He had abandoned them and did not care about them. They were wrong. God cared and always cares for His people. Hear Him:

"Look, their brave men cry aloud in the streets; the envoys of peace weep bitterly. The highways are deserted, no travelers are on the roads. The treaty is broken, its witnesses are despised, no one is respected. The land dries up and wastes away, Lebanon is

ashamed and withers; Sharon is like the Arabah, and Bashan and Carmel drop their leaves. "Now will I arise," says the Lord. "Now will I be exalted; now will I be lifted up" (Isaiah 33:7-10 NIV).

God saw how desperate the people of Israel were and promised them deliverance. He, God was to be exalted, Dear friend, when you pass through tough times, wondering whether your God is good, remember that He is perfect in timing. When the situation around you, in your village, town or country is not the best, and you are wondering where the prayer-answering God has gone, remember that God has a timing that is always perfect. He is seeing. He is watching. He is loving, and He will arise!

At last, Muh got angry, went back to the village and settled there, doing little jobs; his education wasted!

Friend in the Lord, whatever your situation, never throw in the towel. Hang on and wait for God's timely intervention. It will always come at the right time. May your God arise in your situation and bring you His deliverance, in Jesus' Name.

Character Building

Day 35   Character Building

THE GOD OF FIRM BUT LOVING REBUKE!

Many go to church these days wishing to get out feeling happy and loved. Of course, that is God's intention, but His way is neither to bring joy by platitudes nor to only remind us of the great promises on which we should rely for our daily lives. A pastor was living an immoral life with a member of the congregation. He was not happy about it but was just not able to stop. Well, God took him through a series of messages that rebuked him each time he was in the pulpit and he left with a heavy heart that drew him closer to God. When both yielded to the unceasing rebuke of the Word, their deliverances and joy came.

From the Old Testament prophets to Jesus and to the apostles, the message was a rebuke when it had to be, an encouragement when pain needed to be handled, and a teaching when ignorance was the problem. Jesus was not sympathetic when He had to address the religious leaders of the day,

"You snakes! You brood of vipers! How will you escape being condemned to hell?" (Matthew 23:33, NIV), or **"Woe to you, teachers of the law and Pharisees, you hypocrites! You are like whitewashed tombs, which**

look beautiful on the outside but on the inside are full of the bones of the dead and everything unclean" (Matthew 23:27 NIV).

To the Galatians Paul spoke in hard terms: **"You foolish Galatians! Who has bewitched you? Before your very eyes Jesus Christ was clearly portrayed as crucified" (Galatians 3:1 NIV).** The aim of all these rebukes was, and in today's preaching should be, to lead the worshipers to the knowledge of the Truth that would set them free from sin, sorrow, enslavement, spiritual and even physical death. Besides, there is no spiritual growth if there is no repenting from sin and error and becoming more like Christ.

Beloved in the Lord, your life is much better, more peaceful, and more fulfilled when you become more like Jesus. That process involves God rebuking you when you go into His presence to worship with sin, stubbornness or error. When God rebukes you, accept, surrender, obey and worship Him more sincerely. The most blessed worshiper is the repentant Christian. The Christian who blesses the most is the one who becomes more like Christ through obedience and surrender. Whether through encouragement or rebuke, may this be a time of sincere surrender, obedience and wholehearted worship for you, in Jesus' Name.

Day 36   Character Building

LIVE AS TO BE HONORED!

I have been watching short videos on Facebook from time to time. Most of what I see are challenges to unhealthy behavior of which the one who does it eventually harvests the negative consequences. For example, a lady is rude to someone at the gate only to realize when she gets into the office for an interview that the one conducting the interview is the very one she spoke to in total disrespect at the gate, thinking that it was a yard cleaner. Character is everything as far as honor is concerned.

Numerous public figures I have seen seem to fit the same mold. On the one hand were those who were highly honored in office, greatly respected and hailed. But when they left office, they were quite unpopular and hardly received anyone into their homes. The problem was, they were not too friendly, but people went to them for their money and the possibility of getting jobs through them. The other group were those who left office, but their public acclaim and praise did not reduce as much. In this group were those whose connectedness while in office went beyond giving job opportunities. They respected people without discrimination; welcomed people graciously and cared for them sincerely. Their time out of office was still filled with their receiving visits and involvement in people's lives. The first group was respected and appreciated for things done. The second was the group that was honored for who they were. The impact on life is greater in the second group than in the first. While the material things may last, character produced from the encouragement, rebukes, and counsel (from the latter group) had a more lasting impact on life.

One way God honors people is by using them for noble accomplishments for humanity and for His Kingdom and placing them on a platform for respect. So, using the analogy of vessels in the house Paul tells us,

"In a large house there are articles not only of gold and silver, but also of wood and clay; some are for special purposes and some for common use. Those who cleanse themselves from the latter will be instruments for special purposes, made holy, useful to the Master and prepared to do any good work" (2 Timothy 2:20-21 NIV).

Building character is cleansing self for divine use. It makes it pleasurable for God to use you for noble purposes and make you honored by humanity, which creates a greater impact. Oh! How I pray that God will grant you the grace to be of noble character so you will be highly blessed and be a great blessing for others, in Jesus' Name.

Faithfulness & Provision

Day 37   Faithfulness & Provision

WHEN YOU PASS THROUGH THE WATER AND FIRE!

Fires are painful and floods are dangerous, but I am glad that I have passed through them at various times in various ways. I was a little child, running around the farm while my mother was working, and was doing ridge-jumping; skipping over ridges that Mom cultivated. I confidently went off into the air, certain that I would go over a certain ridge. Sadly, I landed on it and got my foot well burnt. Since then, I have always feared fire! Thereafter, I never needed to be told not to play with fire.

As a person who has lived over half a century on earth; as a father, a husband, a student, a teacher, and a pastor, I have tasted the floods of hatred and rancor, the fires of trials and tribulations, the attacks of falsehood and the stings of opposition. I have come out of some stronger and from others very depressed and defeated, but generally these have been times after which I looked back and said, "Lord, thank you. I wonder what I would have been without those times." Yes, I can say for sure that God is honest when He says: **"When you pass through the waters, I will be with you; and when you pass through the rivers, they will not sweep over you. When you walk through the fire, you will not be burned; the flames**

will not set you ablaze. For I am the Lord your God, the Holy One of Israel, your Savior" (Isaiah 43:2-3a NIV). God can keep us from being tempted, molested, oppressed and hard-pressed. Why does He let His children pass through the flood waters and the blazing fires? Let me suggest three reasons:

- Both the flood and the fire purify faith. Sometimes you think that you are a giant of faith; that you know very much and are super strong. That was Peter's situation when he boasted that even if all the other disciples ran away from Jesus during difficult moments, he would never do so. That same night of his confession, he denied Jesus three times. When the reality of his pride came upon him, he wept unto repentance and was able to lead the group to Jesus. Difficult times are God's method of pruning His children.
- Both floods and fire reveal those who are not God's. Faith is tested in adversity. Falsehood and childish faith are revealed in adversity. Jesus' teaching got hard and demanding.

"From this time many of his disciples turned back and no longer followed him. "You do not want to leave too, do you?" Jesus asked the Twelve. Simon Peter answered Him, "Lord, to whom shall we go? You have the words of eternal life" (John 6:66-68 NIV).

Hard teaching, not even the bread of adversity, sent the crowd away except for the Twelve who had nowhere else to go.
- Both floods and fire strengthen faith for those who faithfully allow God to take them through. Israel would almost have had no faith in the Lord had they not passed through the fires of adversity in Egypt, the desert and Babylon. All of Paul's friends and acquaintances abandoned him, but he gave this defense: **"But the Lord stood at my side and gave me strength, so that through me the message might be fully proclaimed and all the Gentiles might hear it. And I was delivered from the lion's mouth"** (2 Timothy 4:17 NIV). Based on that experience, Paul confessed a strong faith in the Lord: **"The Lord will rescue me from every evil attack and will bring me safely to his heavenly kingdom. To him be glory for ever and ever. Amen"** (2 Timothy 4:18 NIV).
- Beloved in the Lord, in the fallen world in which we find ourselves, the floods and fires of life's experiences are not lacking. Child of God, spiritual growth means overcoming weaknesses and becoming like Christ. Allow God to purify you in your times of adversity, so that when He takes you through your waters and fires, your faith will be as strong as a rock, as pure and solid as gold, and your entrance to God's goodness and blessings will be well assured, in Jesus' Name.

Day 38   *Faithfulness & Provision*

LET THE RIGHTEOUS CELEBRATE HIS JUSTICE!

Celebration is the victor's language. It is the victorious who celebrate, but ordinary humanity knows victory only at the end of a battle or after a hard and constraining time. Not so the child of God! God has promised to be with His children, and is always with them, on all occasions and situations. It is both an act of faith and an act of honor to God when you celebrate Him for what you still expect to come to pass.

David, Paul and Silas understood this well and applied it daily. Though David furiously asked God to give his enemies a hard knock on their heads, he spent more time and energy (as viewed in the Psalms), praising God than confronting these enemies. Paul and Silas were well-guarded in a maximum-security prison. They knew the danger and great probability that death lay before them. Yet, **"About midnight Paul and Silas were praying and singing hymns to God, and the other prisoners were listening to them" (Acts 16:25 NIV).** Yes, they knew they served a living God, a triumphant God; One who never fails. He was worthy of such celebration from those who serve and love Him, even when they were in trouble.

Beloved, faith is not just for special people. It is a way of life for the Christian. That is why the Bible tells us that we live by faith and not by sight. Our eyes can deceive us, but our faith cannot. When you face difficult moments, when you face injustice, when people are trampling on your peace and privileges and keeping you away from them, remember who you are to God. **"For we are to God the pleasing aroma of Christ among those who are being saved and those who are perishing" (2 Corinthians 2:15 NIV).** Remember that your life gives God pleasure when you think of Him first and trust Him in all situations. Face injustice and other difficulties with thanksgiving in your heart. Confess like Paul. He went to Troas looking for his friend and brother Titus but did not find him there. He tells us, **"I still had no peace of mind, because I did not find my brother Titus there. So I said goodbye to them and went on to Macedonia. But thanks be to God, who always leads us as captives in Christ's triumphal procession and uses us to spread the aroma of the knowledge of him everywhere" (2 Corinthians 2:13-14 NIV).**

Dear friend, do not wait to find the friend you need, the peace you need, the oneness you need in the family, the freedom you need, or the good exam results you need. You already have God. Celebrate the victory you expect because the God of justice will stand for you, judge your oppressors and give you peace and freedom, in the day of His favor, in Jesus' Name.

Day 39   Faithfulness & Provision

FAITHFULNESS: THE BEST WAY TO PROMOTION!

Do you know people around you whose performance as adults, working in business, administration or other aspects in life, does not surprise you because you could tell from childhood what he or she would be like? One of the ways I remember some of our student leaders from high school days is by hearing their names in positions of responsibility in our society. Faithfulness begets responsibility or promotion.

It is unfortunate when the society observes more bribes and signing into occultic societies to gain professional promotion than they view people being faithful in their responsibilities. Not only do those practices leave the promoted sometimes frustrated in their responsibilities but also leaves the community less developed. The Bible is clear that God puts leaders in place to punish those who do wrong and reward those who do right. Often, corrupt leaders do the opposite. However, God is still in control and has the final say in matters that concern His children. His word stands that, **"Whoever can be trusted with very little can also be trusted with much, and whoever is dishonest with very little will also be dishonest with much"(Luke16:10 NIV).**

Joseph was faithful in his assignment as house boy. God promoted him to manage prisoners, even while he was a prisoner. His management was great and he ended up as Egypt's number two in command, despite being a foreigner and a slave. Against all odds and great opposition, Daniel was promoted from serving the king of Babylon to being a second strong man in the nation. Because he was faithful, God spotted him and moved him up.

Child of God, let your faithfulness in service not be determined by the type and level of your service, or the amount of gain or pay you get. Let your faithfulness be a factor of your faith in the great God who has the final say in the life matters of His children. When God is with you, oppressors are fighting a losing battle, even if the whole society stands against you. Be faithful in the little you have. That is first, a great blessing for those you serve and second, a great way to pave the way for your divine blessings. To be faithful is to be blessed and God will faithfully uphold that in your life, in Jesus' Name.

Day 40   Faithfulness & Provision

THE LORD WILL HEAR YOU!

Prayer can be a risky thing, especially when it is done in public. There are certainly people who wait at occasions to laugh at the one who prays, so they can conclude that the prayer has not been answered. But God hears His own and upholds the faith of those who are trusting in Him enough to pray publicly.

At the ongoing African Nations' cup, the knockout stage that started had been nerve-wracking, tension packed and full of surprises. The goalkeeper for Burkina Faso either out of faith or out of a chosen expression of tension, looked up to heaven and I could imagine he was praying. The journalist I listened to asked repeatedly, "Will his God help him?" When Burkina Faso missed a penalty and Gabon had the opportunity to score and win, my friend was noisy in the house with, "Yes, Gabon, I give you the goal, score and win, you must win..." My heart was raging with passion for that goalkeeper to be honored by God. When Gabon did not score that goal, I took a deep breath and announced without any argument, "I want Burkina Faso to win!" The house was quiet. Thank God there were no Gabonese among us! At last, the Burkinabe goalkeeper did not stop any ball as did the Gabonese keeper. Burkina Faso won the match. Prayer answered!

Beloved, we have a God who answers prayers. Sometimes the road to the answer is long and winding, and even filled with some doubts and anxiety, especially when the waiting has a big impact on one's daily life. There is waiting for answered prayer to get out of the bush, waiting to have a baby after years of marriage, and waiting for an end of war or for your children to be employed in a worsening economy. There is waiting for God to take away your oppressor or your enemy and give you the freedom to feel human, to experience and exercise freedom. Awaiting that which belongs to you by divine designation can sometimes be hard. *Yet, there is no alternative to the time between praying and receiving answers than to wait in faith!*

Beloved, look up to God, trust Him, be patient with Him, and do not allow anxiety, fear, doubt, or weeping to weaken you.

"Rejoice in the Lord always; again I will say, Rejoice…Have no anxiety about anything, but in everything by prayer and supplication with thanksgiving let your requests be made known to God. And the peace of God, which passes all understanding, will keep your hearts and your minds in Christ Jesus." (Philippians 4:4, 6-7 RSV.)

As you pray, rest assured that God has heard; and has taken charge. At the perfect time, God will answer and bless you, in Jesus' Name.

Generosity

WORSHIP YOUR GIVING GOD!

In Africa, we celebrate life and commemorate death by celebrating in food and drink. We were discussing the impending death celebration of a great icon, the people's person that had passed on in our land and concluded that it would be very hectic because he touched just too many lives at individual level and invested in every village in our land. To our shock, another person who was involved in the conversation said, "Who will stay behind rather than coming to a death celebration where there will be much to eat?" After our initial shock, we realized that the generosity of the man who passed on was a major attraction to himself and now to his death. A giving life is a transforming life!

In religion, God or the gods ask for their worshipers to satisfy them by giving to them one thing or the other. The Christian God, however, is the giving God. He makes life and sustains it. He answers prayers and provides for those who trust Him. He gave His Son, that we might have life. That giving is not enough. The Bible says, **"He who did not spare [even] His own Son, but gave Him up for us all, how will He not also, along with Him, graciously give us all things?" (Romans 8:32 AMP).**

Dear friend, what other God can be this sacrificial and loving? What can you do for this great God? Giving Him all your wealth will not be enough because all that you have, from which you give, comes from Him. Worship the Lord. Celebrate His goodness. Honor Him for His generosity and exalt Him who is enthroned above everyone and everything; seated above the heavens and the earth, ruling the universe. What a God! Celebrate Him and be blessed, in Jesus' Name.

Day 42   Generosity

PHILANTHROPY OR GENEROSITY?

It is easy at first sight to take these two words to mean the same thing, but they really do not. We were having a clan monthly meeting, and the national president of the clan's development and cultural association was over a thousand miles away across the ocean. Knowing how much he loved a particular dance and how he loved seeing his people doing things together, I made a short video of the people having a good dance and sent it to him. In a few minutes, the response came that he enjoyed and appreciated the dance, the meeting and all that was going on. Within a few more minutes, he sent a sizeable donation to entertain the people who were present at the occasion. Yes, this was not the first time he did such. He was known for his acts of generosity. His fervent and persistent reaching out to meet needs could have had him described as a philanthropist. This time around, though, it was very special. He was sending the donation from his sick bed in the hospital where he was between life and death. Less than a month from that day, he was pronounced dead. Ah! A generous heart is good.

A philanthropist is "one who makes an active effort to promote human welfare."[5] To be generous is to be "liberal

---

[5] "Philanthropy." *Merriam-Webster.com Dictionary*, Merriam-Webster, http://www.merriam-webster.com/dictionary/philanthropy. Accessed 22 Apr. 2025

in giving, marked by abundance or ample proportions, characterized by a noble or kindly spirit."[6]

Most philanthropists are wealthy people who often establish foundations to which their businesses and other sources of wealth contribute, and to which other people can also contribute. Most of them promote specific causes including care for heart disease and the provision of houses for the poor. Generous people are not necessarily wealthy, but from what they have, they reach out liberally to meet needs and improve human welfare.

- Mostly, if not always, philanthropy is a result of abundance. It is hard to see a philanthropist who is not wealthy or generally very financially successful. In fact, it mostly comes out of extraordinary wealth with which the individuals are not quite sure what to do. Generous people do not give out of the abundance of their bank account as much as the abundance of their hearts of love.
- Sometimes, philanthropists are accused of political agendas. One Western organization, very well known for its philanthropic activities, has often been accused of working to reduce the population of Africa, and its CEO has been shot at with tomatoes in public, in an expression of anger for his activities. Generous people do not have the hearts for bad political agendas

---

[6] "Generous." *Merriam-Webster.com Dictionary*, Merriam-Webster, http://www.merriam-webster.com/dictionary/generous. Accessed 22 Apr. 2025

because their acts are more personal, and they do not do it as part of any organization's requirement.
- Philanthropists hardly feel the pain of giving because it comes out of great abundance. Generous people are often sacrificial, sometimes giving to be left with little or nothing, and then struggle thereafter.
- •Philanthropists make big names, and generous people are sometimes hardly known by people other than those directly touched by their acts.
- •The philanthropist cares more about how to spend his money. He is a humanist. The generous person cares more about how to meet human needs. He is mostly godly in heart and cares for humanity.

Before even rising to prominence, our above-mentioned president did business when he was young, and at a time when most of the elders and age mates from his tribe were first-generation educated people. Most of them who came back home from studying in the West and in other African nations stopped in his house for a few months or years while they looked for a job or to work out their transition into professional life. He has influenced the lives of the political, educational and business elites of his people and the nation. He influenced the lives of the young, the old, male and female alike because he was generous. A big mark of his generosity is visible in his works in the promotion of spirituality. It is very rare to see philanthropists promote spirituality, but generous people do because their hearts are godly and God fearing.

There are two noted rich people in the story of the New Testament. First, **"There was a rich man who was dressed in purple and fine linen and lived in luxury every day. At his gate was laid a beggar named Lazarus, covered with sores and longing to eat what fell from the rich man's table. Even the dogs came and licked his sores" (Luke 16:19-21 NIV).** This man had enough money to have a party every day, but he did not have the heart with which to see the poor, sick beggar at his gate. He did not receive God's approval.

The other rich man: "**At Caesarea there was a man named Cornelius, a centurion in what was known as the Italian Regiment. He and all his family were devout and God-fearing; he gave generously to those in need and prayed to God regularly**" (Acts 10:1-2, NIV). He was God fearing and generous. He gave to the poor. He prayed regularly. At last, God told him through an angel, "**Your prayers and gifts to the poor have come up as a memorial offering before God**" (Acts 10:4b NIV). That is how salvation came to his household and God was established there.

Beloved in the Lord, you can choose to be a philanthropist, but you may have to wait and make it in life first so that your abundance can make a difference in people's lives. Sadly, the absence of God from your heart will leave you without God's approval. When your time comes, humanity might just be celebrating your death, while you are languishing in pain in hell. You can choose to be what God really likes: generous, reaching out to make a difference in people's lives, in small ways and big ways. You may never be known internationally or nationally. But God will bless you as you make the difference in your own little ways. Start today. As you go out this day, pray, "God, help me see and help a needy person today." **Remember, "A generous person will prosper; whoever refreshes others will be refreshed" (Proverbs 11:25 NIV).** Be generous to people, and God will be generous to you in Jesus' Name.

Day 43   *Generosity*

WHAT IS GUIDING YOUR GIVING?

There are many great people today who were made great by the wealthiness and goodness of their parents or close relatives. There are others who were made great by the wealthiness and goodness of others who reached out and made a difference in their lives. Both "parents" and "others" are givers, one just more generous in looking out beyond their own blood relations and seeing needs, not connections. Paradoxically, when you see needs more than you see connections, your giving is a greater blessing to you than you realize.

I grew up to know a very close friend to my uncle. In my young age, I knew them when the two were made "Princes of Mbumland" (our tribe). It is a tribe of over thirty villages, and there is hardly any village that the generosity of these two did not touch. After my uncle left the world stage, the friend continued in even greater measures. Not only did he make his mark by being present in all palaces where there was need or difficulty, providing and ensuring development; he made his mark by touching lives beyond his tribe. I am not sure he knew how many people lived in his house. It is a big home with people, including those of other tribes. He fathered them, sent them to school and prepared them for their future. He was a Christian but in his home were those who practiced Islam and had no blood relation with him yet, he took care of them. He also invited them in a loving, non-pressured manner to trust in Jesus. Sometimes, he just needed a phone call from an unknown voice with a genuine need, and he would give. One of his arguments was, "What if God were to make me the one calling to ask people to give me?" His giving was not guided by blood connections but by need. When he passed away, someone sent condolences to his father, the fon (chief of his village) and another person commented, "To whom should we send condolences for a man who was the son of all villages and father of all?" What a life!

Beloved, when the Bible talks about giving, it often talks of need. Such need-led giving brings blessings for life on earth and in heaven. **"Those who give to the poor will lack nothing, but those who close their eyes to them receive many curses" (Proverbs 28:27 NIV).** Some even close their eyes to the poor in their family! Givers, especially those meeting needs, never lack because God blesses them as His channels. To the rich young man Jesus said, **"If you want to be perfect, go, sell your possessions and give to the poor, and you will have treasure in heaven. Then come, follow me" (Matthew 19:21 NIV).** Giving to meet needs lays for you treasures in heaven, blessings for the life hereafter.

Dear friend in the Lord, God blesses you for humanity and His Kingdom. Therefore,

- Give to take care of your family members: children and others but let that not limit your guide to giving.

- Give to make your mark in your professional world and the social milieu, but do not let selfish considerations guide and end your giving;
- See the need beyond your house; reach out to give some meaning to people's lives; reach out to build God's Kingdom. The truth still stands today: **"In everything I did, I showed you that by this kind of hard work we must help the weak, remembering the words the Lord Jesus himself said: 'It is more blessed to give than to receive'" (Acts 20:35 NIV).**

When you work hard and are blessed to have, do not see the weak as lazy beggars but as needy people sent to you by God. Reach out to their needs, and be blessed here and hereafter, in Jesus' Name.

Day 44 — *Generosity*

DO NOT EAT WITHOUT SOWING!

The African Nations' Cup competition was moving to the knockout stage. Some nations were celebrating while others were going home sadly eliminated. That is life. One of the things that caught my attention in this competition was that almost all the players were professionals, playing mostly out of Africa. Before this, there were some local players in the team at competitions like this one. European clubs would come to the competition to look for players. What changed? Are African nations eating without sowing for the future?

In Cameroon the National Football Cup Finals was not played for at least two years. In 2021, PWD Bamenda (a first division club), qualified for the finals, trained for sixteen months and camped in the capital, Yaoundé, for about a month. The year ended without that cup finals played. When the local competition is so ignored, set apart or mismanaged, how will the players sell themselves to professional clubs for the country to fetch for future national team competitions? Eating without sowing is shooting oneself in the foot!

Paul gives a very simple but powerful instruction, **"The one who is unwilling to work shall not eat" (2 Thessalonians 3:10 NIV).** Work produces the fruit we eat. But eating without working is a prominent problem:

Countries owe huge debts because they borrow. They do not invest but consume. Sometimes the money ends up in private hands and in private accounts back in the country from which the money was borrowed.

- Individuals borrow without investing and soon find themselves having to shy away from the people they owe.
- People work and then retire without anything with which to care for themselves in the time of their deserved rest. Some end up dying early, out of frustration.
- People lead institutions like churches, businesses, and even nations without thinking about what happens to the institution when they are gone. When they leave to retire or die the institution folds up.

Beloved in the Lord,

- May the Lord grant you grace to not eat your seed.
- May the Lord grant you grace to sow such that you can eat far into the future.
- May the Lord enrich the works of your hands so that the enemy does not make them fruitless.
- May the Lord give you investment ideas and opportunities.
- May the Lord revive and finish any of your investments that are at a standstill.
- May the Lord enable you to sow in lives for the future of your institution.

- May the Lord enable you to pay all your debts.
- May the Lord teach you to live within your means and be contented with what you have while trusting Him for more. That is the highway to eating and sowing.

Above all, be sure you keep eating from the Bible, the spiritual food that God took four hundred years and forty people to put together for you and me. It is the dining table for life's best investments. It is the greatest source of all the best blessings for you and through you. Eat it daily and be blessed and bless others, in Jesus' Name.

Jehovah-Jireh

Day 45   Jehovah-Jireh

LET GOD GIVE YOU LIFE!

It is interesting that though different cultures talk differently about what happens after death, all cultures trace life back to God. There are just three well-known monotheistic "religions" (those that believe there is one God) in the world: Judaism, Christianity and Islam. Yet even the religions that believe in the existence of multiple gods still attribute creation to one of them. Professor Imasogie, a Nigerian Christian theologian, for example, explains African religious beliefs as holding to a bureaucratic monotheism, meaning that there is one "God" who operates through many deities (small gods) in administering life and taking care of humanity. All point to the fact that the origin of life is God. The Bible is not a book written to *argue* for the existence of God or seek to convince anyone about Him or about life itself. The Bible is God speaking to the people He has created and giving them directives on how to relate with Him and with each other. So, it simply states without argument, **"In the beginning God created the heavens and the earth" (Genesis 1:1 NIV).**

I have had the privilege of living in the poorest situations and at least, living among the rich. I have experienced life in the undeveloped parts of the world and dined a few times with the super blessed of the earth. I have come to the conclusion that there are only two major differences between all humanity of all races, colors, classes, status and cultures. Some live more comfortably than others and some live much longer than others. That is all! Everyone is created by God and comes to the earth through birth by a woman. Each goes through different life opportunities and experiences, but all die, no matter how. All are buried or burnt into ashes and leave the stage of life on earth, no matter how indispensable they have been in their circles of influence. More seriously, they take away nothing, not even a pin from their abundance or the best possession from their lack. Job's reaction to his loss was wise and informative, **"Naked I came from my mother's womb, and naked I will depart. The Lord gave and the Lord has taken away; may the name of the Lord be praised" (Job 1:21 NIV).**

Beloved, if God can take away as He did to Job, and give back as He gave to Job; if God can provide and withhold both the things of life and above all, life itself, how can it be wisdom for anyone to attribute his or her life to anyone or anything else? King Solomon experienced great wisdom, possession and position.

"King Solomon was greater in riches and wisdom than all the other kings of the earth. All the kings of the earth sought audience with Solomon to hear the

wisdom God had put in his heart" (2 Chronicles 9:22-23 NIV).

No one ever since has had such wisdom, attention, and possession. Yet, when Solomon reflected on his life, the recurrent theme was **"Meaningless! Meaningless!" says the Teacher. "Utterly meaningless! Everything is meaningless" (Ecclesiastes 1:2 NIV).** And his conclusion was simple but profound and weighty, **"Now all has been heard; here is the conclusion of the matter: Fear God and keep his commandments, for this is the duty of all mankind" (Ecclesiastes 12:13 NIV).** Now we speak of Solomon in history. The wise, rich and famous King Solomon died!

Beloved in the Lord:

▪ Do not trust comfort for life. Trust God for your comfort.

▪ Do not seek a long life of comfort; seek a quality life of submission to God and His ways. No matter how comfortable or uncomfortable you are; regardless of how long you live, you will die and God, God alone knows how and when, because He alone brought you to the earth and will take you out of it, without negotiating with you or anyone else.

May God, *not your situation*, be your comfort, your peace, and your life, now and always; in Jesus' Name.

Love

Day 46   *Love*

CELEBRATE GOD AS LOVE

Life can be complicated. It was easy for me to think or even conclude that my father did not love me. He did not do certain things I expected of him and did some things I did not expect him to do. What I did not realize was that he was struggling with deep personal issues and my own behavior did not help the situation either. Much later in life we both came to some understanding of our situations, and I realized that love does not mean receiving what you want or always needing or being pampered irrespective of what you are or do.

God's love for us is very much blurred by the struggles and difficulties, oppressions, sufferings, killings, hunger, and all other problems we go through at the personal, local and global level. How can a loving God watch all these problems and do nothing when He has all the power to do as He wills? Does He not will human happiness? Is it true as an unbelieving friend said to me, that "God is helpless before Satan"? How can a loving God send people to hell, or is hell just a concept to frighten people to morality? Yet, the Bible says in very straight and simple terms, **"God is love..." (1 John 4:16b NIV)**. In nature and character God is love. So, why is there pain in and all around us? As complicated as the problem of evil is, we can observe a few things:

1. In His love and impartiality, God has set principles by which the world operates. If unbelievers live in accordance with those principles, they experience God's grace and love. For example, the same principles work in business and investment for all, including believers and unbelievers. If an unbeliever uses Biblical principles to do business, he excels. If a believer prays and acts against those principles, he loses. That is God's impartiality. God is love.

2. God has told us the truth, His will, in terms of both means and results. When humanity acts contrary to the means as individuals, small groups or even globally, they will reap the unhealthy results.

"And so we know and rely on the love God has for us. God is love. Whoever lives in love lives in God, and God in them. This is how love is made complete among us so that we will have confidence on the day of judgment: In this world we are like Jesus" (1 John 4:16-17 NIV).

Love is made complete among us when we live in love. When we live in love, God is in us. If we confess Jesus, we should live like Him and spread love. That too is a principle to follow.

3. God has set eternity in view and has made it clear that there is a day of judgment. If people obey principles here

without Christ, at first they will make it in many ways, get profits, live a better life and excel. But they will be easily exploitative, selfish, and unloving. China and France are most glaring examples. Many individuals within our communities are like these two nations. Second, if they obey principles without Christ, they will face judgment and lose eternity. God in His love and justice has made clear the results before the exams. He who chooses to go to hell cannot blame God.

4. God enabled love after Adam and Eve disobeyed and invited sin into the human race. Sin destroyed love. God so loved the world that He became man (in Christ) and died to give humanity the ability to live in love and to follow Him. God laid down principles for life on earth and beyond. He who rejects Christ cannot know God, see His love or keep His principles without exploiting and oppressing others. **"Now this is eternal life: that they know you, the only true God, and Jesus Christ, whom you have sent" (John 17:3 NIV).**

Beloved, if indeed you have given your life to God through Christ:

- Celebrate Him. He loves you and will deliver you from the hands of those who oppress and disfavor you. Keep in step with Him and be patient.
- Pray for grace for your people and the world to know and follow divinely set principles for life. Also pray they will accept Jesus as their Savior and Lord so that they

can love humanity, be positive in their community and make it to heaven.
- Remember that you are like Christ in this world. Preach like Christ and live like Him. Then, you will be blessed and be a blessing to many as you cause them to join you celebrating God and His love, in Jesus' Name.

Day 47 — Love

SOCIAL CAPITAL IS INVESTED NOT EXPLOITED!

I worked in an environment where there were many young people. After a few years, I could identify two groups of those who related with me. The first group consisted of those who came to ask for assistance. I only saw them when they were in need. Of course, I helped when I could, but it was never easy. The second group consisted of those who came to help without asking for any assistance even though they had needs. Some came to clean my clothes, others to cut the grass and keep the compound clean, and some even offered to go help with farm work. Which of these two do you think caught my attention? Of course, the second! Which of these do you think I remember years after, and can still turn to help them even when they have not asked? You are right again; it is the second group! *In your social life do not raise helpers, raise friends!*

You build friends when you care about their lives more than you think about how they can meet your needs. You build fruitful friends when you think of ways to make their lives better (even if they have more than you) instead of how they can make your life better. You build social capital when you think more about friendship than about "people-treasures you can exploit." It looks strange but David was making a very strong statement about the value he attached to the lives of those who mattered to him.

"David longed for water and said, 'Oh, that someone would get me a drink of water from the well near the gate of Bethlehem!' So the three mighty warriors broke through the Philistine lines, drew water from the well near the gate of Bethlehem and carried it back to David. But he refused to drink it; instead, he poured it out before the Lord. 'Far be it from me, Lord, to do this!' he said. 'Is it not the blood of men who went at the risk of their lives?' And David would not drink it. Such were the exploits of the three mighty warriors" (2 Samuel 23:15-17 NIV).

Yes, David was in need! Yes, these men loved him enough to risk their lives to bring him some water to drink. But David's action is saying their lives are more important than the quenching of his taste. You are building good friends who will stick out their necks for you when they can see that you are a friend who cares about them, rather than you are just exploiting them for your future.

Dear friend in the Lord, there is a paradox here you have to manage well. It is this: you build friends or social capital knowing that it will make a difference in your life, but your real focus in building those relationships is not so much what you will benefit as much as just the relationship in which you are ready to give. You never give in order to receive but in giving you are *likely* to receive. Christ's way is to reach out sacrificially, build friendship caringly, and reject the opportunity to exploit wholeheartedly and lovingly. That is an investment in social capital that will bless you and make you a blessing. Invest, do not exploit; then you will reap without destroying, in Jesus' Name.

Day 48 *Love*

DO NOT THROW AT, REACH OUT TO!

It is so natural to be a boss rather than to reach out to those who we have the privilege to influence positively. My good friend was a stepson. His mother had him before getting married but happily brought him along to her marital home. The husband welcomed him with the mother and at first, it looked good. We were having a great time until somehow the stepfather became wild, unloving, rash and quite rude. One day he wondered aloud about who gave birth to this stupid stubborn boy. Before he knew it, the boy packed his things, left and returned to his mother's village where he grew up without a father. The good thing is this boy turned out to be the most responsible of the mother's children and is taking great care of her. When fathers and mothers become bosses over their children, or over their housemates, they transfer such attitudes to managing businesses, offices and the nation. It takes grace for such children to grow and not be bitter enough to attempt revenge or transfer aggression to others.

Beloved, do you know that you could be creating a problem for a whole nation by maltreating that young person working for you as house help, servant in the office, driver, junior staff, or volunteer in the church? The fact that you have anyone working for you means that you are in need! *Do not see the money you give him or her as more important than the services you receive!*

God has given you the grace to care for an orphan or for a child belonging to a family member. Reach out in love and mercy to him or her. Throwing things at the child with a twisted face, giving tuition with a grumbling mind, or feeding the child with the words, "I am just wasting my food," is sowing discord in that child and making her look like a semi-person or a thing. If that child is successful in life, you will be too ashamed to take anything from him or her. If the child becomes embittered enough to become a social danger, you will likely be the first victim. *Ignoring to assist or throwing help out is an act of compulsion. Reaching out to make someone's life better is an act of love.* Though costly, love always wins at last.

In need of a baby, Sarah impressed her husband to take her slave girl Hagar for a wife. Abraham did so and Hagar became pregnant. Unfortunately, Hagar became arrogant and despised Sarah and Sarah became rash, harsh and oppressive enough for Hagar to flee the household. On the way to nowhere, she met an angel who told her to go back. He said to her: **"You are now pregnant, and you will give birth to a son. You shall name him Ishmael, for the Lord has heard of your misery" (Genesis 16:11 NIV).** This moment was an ultimate life experience for Hagar. It wiped away her tears and in her response to God, **"She gave this name to the Lord who spoke to her: 'You are the God who sees me,' for she said, 'I have now seen the One who sees me'" (Genesis 16:13 NIV).**

Beloved in The Lord,

If you are throwing out "help" instead of giving love or if you are oppressing junior staff more than assisting them to grow, remember that God sees and cares for the oppressed! Ishmael (Hagar's son) became a thorn in the flesh of Sarah's descendants! Please do not set fire to follow the children you are painfully bringing up with your sweat.

If you are oppressed, looked down on, or are having things thrown at, including slangs, look up to God. Know that you are passing by and respond in the most loving way possible. Submitting even as a slave is not a sign of weakness, it is a winning strategy. It is the living of a loving heart, and a reaching out to receive God's love. Humility, love and a refusal to retaliate is taking the highway to being blessed and blessing others. In your home, class, marketplace, and office, build a loving environment. That will give us a blessed nation. God so loved you that He did not throw salvation at you, He reached out to you with His Son and saved you. Do likewise, reach out in love and be blessed and be a blessing, in Jesus' Name.

Day 49 *Love*

OVERCOMING HURT TO CARE!

Bearing one another's burdens means caring, and caring has many obstacles, including hurt. How do you care for someone who has hurt you and the pain of his or her actions is still freshly present? One of the greatest "hurt and lack of care" examples is in the relationship of "Mr. Soh" and his wife. They were married for decades, slept on the same bed, went out the same door but unfortunately, didn't communicate. Mr. Soh had a painful death of a very close blood relative and went to the village without informing his wife. The wife got news of it and traveled by herself separately. They met in the village, buried and came back the same way they went, each alone. One of the biggest events of Soh's life happened in the absence of his wife. Imagine that as they traveled for the funeral, one had an accident. Would she or he call the partner? The explanation of each of them for their actions was simply, "I am very angry with what he or she has done to me." Of course, there will be deep hurts in our sinful world, but how can we put aside such hurts in order to care?

We can follow the example of God. Humanity had hurt God deeply when Adam and Eve disobeyed Him in the Garden of Eden, and that spirit of disobedience continued in the rest of humanity. God could have condemned the human race and wiped it out. No! He did not. Instead, God loved the world so He gave His Son to die and set us free. He laid aside His hurt and saved us. Interestingly, God did not do it for what we would bring to Him. He is totally sufficient in Himself. It was, therefore, His interest in our joy and peace that made Him send His Son to die for us. Paul was beaten, considered dead, and thrown out of the city. He got up and walked back there to minister. How could he do that? He says in **Philippians 2:3-4 NIV: "Do nothing out of selfish ambition or vain conceit. Rather, in humility value others above yourselves, not looking to your own interests but each of you to the interests of the others."** Paul is saying:

- Do not do anything (including care) with selfish reasons. Do not think of what you will gain. Do not be selfish.
- Do nothing out of pride. If you care so that you can be seen as a great man who does things, it will be hard to reach out to someone who has hurt you because you may not talk proudly about it.
- Be humble. Humility gives us the grace to do things extraordinarily. Humility means not considering yourself higher than you ought. That enables you to care for even someone far below your level.
- Look to the interest of others. It is surprising Paul does not say look to the needs of others, but to their interests. If you can watch to see the interests of others, what about their needs? It will be easier for you to care for their needs.

Beloved, on the journey of life, love, humility and selflessness are aspects of life that can enable care even when you are hurt and angry. When hurt, pray for the Spirit, your Comforter, who is in your heart to comfort you. Then, pray for God to fill your heart with love. Why? **"Above all, love each other deeply, because love covers over a multitude of sins" (1 Peter 4:8 NIV).** Let love soften your heart towards the person who has hurt you and strengthen your hands and feet to care for that person. That is grace. You have received grace from God. Give it out and be blessed, in Jesus' Name.

Day 50   Love

MORE THAN RULES: RELATE!

Have you sometimes wondered why there is so much talk of Christianity and so little substance in terms of actual living of the Christian life? How is it that we have corrupt Christians, sexually perverted Christians, and people who are in church on Sunday shouting "Hallelujah" to Jesus who are also thieves in the night? There are many reasons, including the fact that there are many unbelievers in the church today. There is one reason, not commonly spoken but silently promoted by many, which I believe is the most deceptive, hiding many hypocrites. It is "Christianity" built on worldly principles, particularly rules and regulations.

There are some serious "don'ts" of the modern Christian message that are often preached and disobeyed nearly even more: a Christian woman should not dress in short skirts or wear trousers, a good Christian man should not drink alcohol or bring it to the churchyard, she or he should not commune with unbelievers, and should not take or give bribes, among others. We may add the positive ones including a good Christian should always be in church and at Bible studies and give his or her tithes. Why are these rules so difficult to obey? By themselves, they are worldly principles grossly incapable of stopping people from doing them.

"Since you died with Christ to the elemental spiritual forces of this world, why, as though you still belonged to the world, do you submit to its rules: 'Do not handle! Do not taste! Do not touch!?' These rules, which have to do with things that are all destined to perish with use, are based on merely human commands and teachings. Such regulations indeed have an appearance of wisdom, with their self-imposed worship, their false humility and their harsh treatment of the body, but they lack any value in restraining sensual indulgence" (Colossians 2:20-23 NIV).

As good as the rules of "dos and don'ts" look, they lack the power of the Spirit. Unfortunately, many are in church who live by those rules and regulations. Those who are able to keep many of them easily become overtaken by a "holier than thou" pride, while those who fail to keep many of them just drag themselves along with others, with little or no joy in Christianity.

Jesus' summary of the greatest commitment is a perfect summary of Christianity: *Love!* When you love God with all your heart, you will do things that make Him happy with you rather than avoid things that will lead you to hell. Of course, love for God will mold you to detest things that would make God unhappy enough to send you to hell. If you love your neighbor, you will seek his or her best, rather than steal from him or her, destroy his daughter in immorality, dress in a way that can seduce him, or bribe your child into a position that your neighbor's child should be occupying. If you love yourself, you will be engaged in things that will build up your spirituality, build your body, your family, and your career, and keep away from things that endanger you. That is how you escape indulging in practices including alcohol and immorality. That is why you will be passionate about being there for Bible study, prayer meetings and Sunday services: to grow. That is how you will keep yourself free from immorality, corruption, cheating and from the danger of falling into the hands of both humans and God. Yes,

"The commandments, 'You shall not commit adultery,' 'You shall not murder,' 'You shall not steal,' 'You shall not covet,' and whatever other command there may be, are summed up in this one command: 'Love your neighbor as yourself.' Love does no harm to a neighbor. Therefore, love is the fulfillment of the law" (Romans 13:9-10 NIV).

Beloved in the Lord, if you have not given your life to Jesus, no number of laws, rules or regulations will help you to be a good person and live an admirable life that will please God. If you have given your life to Jesus, instead of remaining at the low "law level" of life, develop a close relationship with Jesus and a strong relationship with people. Connect with God and read His word. The law in His word and in society will help you know what is wrong.

The Holy Spirit in you will empower you and give you that Fruit that will help you withstand temptations and live a life of care for yourself, your neighbor, and God and His things. Obedient Christianity is not a product of rules and regulations but of love. Relate well. Love God and humanity and you will overcome the things that rules and regulations try to keep you from doing. Then, you will be blessed and be a great blessing to others, in Jesus' Name.

God's Guidance

Day 51   God's Guidance

TOUCH THE EARTH FROM HEAVEN!

It was a surprise to me when I saw a western movie in which a living human being was communicating with the dead. The old woman lived in the countryside by herself but whenever she needed counsel, she would go into a hut that looked like their storeroom, a little isolated from the house. She would sit down and call on her late husband who came and spoke to her, giving her counsel on issues for which she needed assistance. As long as that hut was locked, she had no access to the husband, yet the husband did not live in that hut. The hut was just their place of meeting. In most cultures, there is a recognition of the need for a voice of counsel from beyond. The question is where is that beyond and how do we get the voice from there?

The most difficult thing a Christian faces, which is at the same time a great jewel of the Christian faith, is that Christians are citizens of heaven living on earth. In making a distinction between the unbeliever and Christian, Paul says, **"Their mind is set on earthly things. But our citizenship is in heaven" (Philippians 3:19b-20a NIV).** Note the place of the mind because the Bible would come again to tell the Christian living on earth to, **"Set your**

minds on things above, not on earthly things" (Colossians 3:2 NIV). If the believer would make a significant impact on life on earth, he or she must have the mind of Christ above and use it to interpret reality and influence humanity in a godly way. The good thing is, God speaks into all things, gives guidance in all things as we trust Him and desires to reach humanity through the mind of Christ in the believer.

Dear friend, life makes so much difference when it is viewed with the mind of Christ, interpreted in the wisdom of God and lived in the guidance of the Holy Spirit, the Spirit of truth. When you have allowed Christ to take full control of your life, then, your mind is not ordinary. **"Who has known the mind of the Lord so as to instruct him?" But we have the mind of Christ" (1 Corinthians 2:16 b NIV):** For the mind that can touch the earth from heaven, give your life to Christ and have the mind of Christ, without which you cannot think heavenly.

- To keep and perpetually operate in the mind of Christ, always stay close to His word, reading and meditating on it. **"Let the message of Christ dwell among you richly as you teach and admonish one another…" (Colossians 3:16a, NIV).**
- Because the world is tempting and will continuously try to draw you to itself away from heaven, **"… walk by the Spirit, and you will not gratify the desires of the flesh" (Galatians 5:16 NIV).**

God is not as far away from humanity as it seems. God lives in His children. Those who submit to Him will touch the world with their heavenly minds and bring enormous good to those around them and beyond. Give your heart to Jesus and have such great influence, in Jesus' Name.

Day 52 — God's Guidance

JUST FOLLOW AND YOU WILL BE FINE!

Have you ever lost your way and had to struggle back to the right way? Three of us were out for a long journey from school to our village. It was our first time on that road, and we depended on one of us who told us he knew the way. We started well but along the way in the forest, we got to a junction and our friend who "knew the road" was as lost as we were. We stood there for some time, with no one around to help. So, we decided to take one of the two roads before us. Before we knew it, we were going further and further into the forest, in an unrecognizable environment. It took us about an hour to figure out that we were lost. We came back, followed the right way and got home.

As I thought back at this experience, I also noticed that I had some good friends who got into some confusion in their lives and took directions that led them to unfortunate ends. Some ended that way because they wanted to avoid struggling, look for easy ways out of things and have a quick enjoyable life. Others simply refused to listen to advice from our elders and in one case, the intelligent boy finished secondary school and with no explanation, just refused to go to high school. Decision-making can be difficult, especially when you are at a crossroads. God knows that very well. As God who knows all things, sees all things and understands all things, He guides in all things as well. He told Israel that in their time of difficulties when they wondered what to do, there would be teachers for them, and **"Whether you turn to the right or to the left, your ears will hear a voice behind you, saying, 'This is the way; walk in it'" (Isaiah 30:21 NIV).** The certainty of God's leadership is that the results are sure and best.

Today, dear friend, call on God to guide you. Sit in His presence in prayer and have a roadmap for this week. Should you get into any uncertainty as to what to do with yourself, your business, family, or any area of your involvement that creates uncertainties, ask God for a clear direction of what to do. Directly through His word or indirectly through someone, God will show you what to do, what direction to take, and it will be well with you. May the Lord keep you, guide you and lead you to the best for you and your family, in Jesus' Name.

Day 53   God's Guidance

GOD IS YOUR EVER-PRESENT GUIDE!

As the sun went down on the African Nations' Cup competition, AFCON 2021, people left with lots of stories, regrets, accusations, and celebrations. My mind goes to Egypt and particularly to Carlos Queiroz. It must have been very painful for this man, Egypt's coach, watching his team from the crowd, rather than being there to give them necessary corrections and encouragements during the match. Unfortunately for him, he was not able to jump down to the pitch smiling the way he ran out of the waiting room after Egypt beat Cameroon in the semi-finals, as he was red carded. Egypt lost the cup! What a guide!

The players, the nation (Egypt), and his friends and family would have felt much more pain. When your coach receives a red card and is dismissed from the field, though there are assistants, some guidance is missing. This presents both physical and psychological setbacks for the team. Second, one would wonder what kind of example he gives to the players. A good guide in life gives both skill and integrity because the marriage of these two is critical for a successful and peaceful life.

Child of God, two things can be learned from this story:

- You have a guide in life who never fails and will never fail you. He can never receive a red card from anyone for He has the final say in all things. Allow God to guide you, for He is always ready, loving and willing to guide you to your best in life. As long as you remain faithfully obedient to Him, **"The Lord will guide you always; he will satisfy your needs in a sun-scorched land and will strengthen your frame. You will be like a well-watered garden, like a spring whose waters never fail" (Isaiah 58:11 NIV).**

- God does not just give you skills but provides character too. He will help you accomplish the things He has called you to do in life, especially professionally. He will also build your character, which helps you to have good relationships and ensure your entrance to heaven. You will never lose in life because God, your Coach and Mentor was not there. Never! He will never leave you nor forsake you. The example and teaching He gives you on life is always worth following.

Beloved in the Lord, as God guides and grants you success today and always, remember that He will make you "like a well-watered garden, like a spring whose waters never fail." Be a blessing to others and God will bless you. May God guide and bless you throughout your lifetime, so the flow of blessings to you, and from you to those around you never cease, in Jesus' Name.

LET GOD LEAD

Decision-making about what to do in life is not always easy. I found myself on the way to Yaoundé when I passed my high school exams; the A/L GCE. The problem was, I was not sure if I was in that car because my uncle had come home and could take me along, or because I really wanted to go to this lone university in Cameroon, which was dominantly in French. I desired to be an agricultural economist, but I did not know that the university did not offer that subject area to study. I spent two years before God redirected me to a different school to do what I so desired, even if I still would not end up in the same field. When it comes to a career, let God lead you. Let God lead your children even if it's through you.

The people Jesus chose for His disciples were gainfully involved professionally. Fishing was big business and Peter was a fisherman. Matthew was a tax collector or treasury officer, and the other disciples worked in various areas. It was a big career shift for each of them. Luke was still a medical doctor but served well in the work of missions. When Jesus died, Peter was tempted to return to fishing with the others because he did not see how they would continue without Jesus Christ. Jesus showed up and got them back to the missionary assignment. To let God lead you or yours:

- Love Him. Without love it is hard to hear God's guidance because the world's voices are very loud. The voices including money, prestige, and popularity are loud in calling people toward careers, but these voices may not lead to sustained joy and satisfaction. It is hard to hear God lead in a direction you do not like, unless you love Him and want to glorify Him. God has left each of us on earth for a purpose. The career you choose is essential in fulfilling your purpose. Choose your career, or carry out what you now do, as an expression of your love for God.
- Check your burdens. The Psalmist says, **"Praise be to the Lord, to God our Savior, who daily bears our burdens" (Psalm 68:19 NIV).** God is perpetually concerned with the things that burden us; the things that disturb us. But how does He express that care?
- Through His children. Through a caring doctor God keeps or returns you to good health. Through a good farmer God feeds your body and you are not poisoned by how the food is handled. Through a good seamstress God dresses you. From what burdens do you want God to use you to help others in life? Does your heart go out for the sick? Then consider being a medical doctor or a counselor. Does your heart ache when you see people being oppressed? Then consider being a lawyer or a judge.
- Consider your giftedness. What you can do is an indicator of what God desires to do with you. But

remember that each of us has multiple abilities. Being a scientist means you can be in the medical field, engineering, and agriculture among other things. Ability should be guided by God's revelation, especially through the burdens in your heart.

Beloved in the Lord, in all things pray and seek God's direction. Through His Word and His Spirit, He will confirm His call upon your life and enable you to help your children make right decisions and choices. Remember the multi-millionaire in East Africa who heard God and sold off his businesses and began to care for street children. Now, he has transformed the lives of thousands of kids. Do not just sing it, but believe God is serious when He says, "**'For I know the plans I have for you,' declares the Lord, 'plans to prosper you and not to harm you, plans to give you hope and a future'" (Jeremiah 29:11 NIV).** Your life will be most fulfilled if it is in His plan. Help your child to have a fulfilled professional life by enabling the child to find his or her way in God's plan for his or her life. Being in God's career plan is a highway to being blessed and blessing others. God is there to show you. Do not miss it, in Jesus' Name.

God's Plans

Day 55 God's Plans

CELEBRATE HE WHO HAS THE FINAL SAY

Life can be very frustrating when you look around, all you see is danger and you do not know how to handle it or even how you will get out of it. As children, there were times when even our play turned violent and the strong guy in the group started to bully and play rough. The easiest way to stop him was often using the promise, "We will tell Daddy!" He stopped when he knew he was wrong, but he continued when he thought he was right. Father often judged correctly the one who was right and gave out punishment where it was necessary.

When Israel faced trouble as a nation, they knew that their God was there. He was the God of Israel, to whom they could turn at all times. He was not the God of the mountain or of the plain, but the God of the earth. He never disappointed them. When the spies went to have a look at Jericho, Rahab took care of them because she knew what their God had done and could do. She told them,

"We have heard how the Lord dried up the water of the Red Sea for you when you came out of Egypt, and what you did to Sihon and Og, the two kings of the Amorites east of the Jordan, whom you completely destroyed.

When we heard of it, our hearts melted in fear and everyone's courage failed because of you, for the Lord your God is God in heaven above and on the earth below" (Joshua 2:10-11 NIV).

She was right!

Beloved in the Lord, that same God is Father of our Lord Jesus Christ. He has not changed. If you trust in Jesus, He is your God, mighty in battle and great in power. Though the world quakes and the great nations roar, though your enemies roar at you and want to make your heart quake in fear and anticipation of their success, remember that the God you serve is the God of all the earth. He has the final say in all things. Call on Him. Hand over all situations to Him and remember, **"He says, 'Be still, and know that I am God; I will be exalted among the nations, I will be exalted in the earth'" (Psalm 46:10 NIV).** In your stillness, in your calmness of heart and mind, worship Him. Celebrate Him, for whatever the world around you holds, God will speak in your favor and bless you, in Jesus' Name.

Day 56   *God's Plans*

GOD HAS THE PLAN: FOLLOW HIM!

On a Sunday, March 28th, after waiting for the fourth round, my father was told, "It's a boy!" Knowing him well enough, I can imagine him smiling broadly and breathing in words, "He-eh, hehem" before concluding "We thank God." But my tribute today goes to Fai Warr, the sub-chief during whose reign I was born and who had the grace of giving me the name Bungansa. I have always thought that he gave me a name that might have affected me negatively: Bungansa means, "without a lawyer." But this night, I had a revelation.

The man was in conflict with the palace of the village of my birth, the fon under whom Fai Warr was a sub-chief. Apparently, the conflict was protracted, and he was not getting it settled. So, at my birth he voiced it out in a very memorable way, "I [we] do not have a lawyer to defend us in this, our clear case." I remember that I was in my forties when he carried me on his lap (not common in our culture) and told the story to men and women packed full in his palace sitting room (kibuh). He ended with a smile, telling us that only a few months after he named me, and within the same year, the case was over and Nsame "the case is over" was born to our closest neighbor in the village. So, Bungansa was not a regret but a cry of desperation to God! It's like saying, "Father God, I do not have a lawyer, take over my case." Then quickly and effectively God did, and it soon was over. Amen!

A colleague minister observed to me once, "Doc, from when I knew you, your things are always hard to get through, but they eventually do!" The important part is they eventually do, because while the enemies may fight your course in life, when God is your lawyer, He pushes them out of the way and gives you success. After all, He has the master plan of your life and ensures that it works out well.

In the turns and twists of my life, I have discovered that God's ways are not my ways, but God's ways are for my ways and my ultimate good. In the desperations and joys of my life, I have realized that His grace sustains and delivers me from every disgrace. In my intricacies and simplicities of life, I have discovered that it is neither how intelligent I am nor how stupid I am that paves or blocks my progress. It is however how much I allow God to make the decisions and lead me to my next turn in life. In the strife and struggles of my life, I have realized that the interventions of heaven produce more than all the best lawyers of the world put together can do. Hallelujah!

The next time you feel lonely and helpless enough to think your name may, even temporarily be "Bungansa," remember to look up to heaven, raise your hands and tell God, "Father, I do not have any lawyer, please take control." Then sit back, relax, and watch what God will do for you.

Do not forget in any situation that the plan of your life was drawn before the creation of the world. That God has a plan for you, for your future, to give you hope and victory, is not the end. He also says, **"From the east I summon a bird of prey; from a far-off land, a man to fulfill my purpose. What I have said, that I will bring about; what I have planned, that I will do" (Isaiah 46:11 NIV).** God plans. God upholds. God sustains and brings to accomplishment in His own way.

Beloved in the grace of God, may the Lord stand for you, fight for you, establish His will for your life and take you to its fulfillment for His glory, your blessing, and the blessing of all humanity, in Jesus' Name.

Day 57 — God's Plans

CELEBRATE YOUR BUILDER!

I assisted at the removal of the corpse of a young, vibrant, and hard-working man, "Ngom" from our quarter who passed away. Ngom had picked up a boy basically from the street and brought him to his mechanic garage and trained him. The young man had lost both parents and considered Ngom his father. In addition to helping him become professional, Ngom also helped him to build a personal house here in town. You can imagine how some of Ngom's friends saw him as a foolish man who wasted his resources on someone who was not related to him. What we had known of Ngom, among other things, was that he did not have people in his family who stood for him, and he sounded lonely. He left behind a young wife and kids. So, who takes over the care of the children in particular? The young man he trained is very responsible and loving enough to care for the kids. God sees, knows, and plans our future before it comes.

God's ways are not our ways. They are higher, better and more profitable, not for Him but for us. Being God means being totally self-satisfied, totally independent of anything, not changeable, knowing all things and capable of doing anything He wants. He uses these qualities to bring us to life and to build our lives for the better. He is perpetual and trustworthy. He does not fail, though we may not always see it. He carries out His plans for you, especially when you obey Him. **"Many are the plans in a person's heart, but it is the Lord's purpose that prevails. The fear of the Lord leads to life" (Proverbs 19:21, 23a NIV).**

Dearly loved of God, despite all the investments that you have made or are making, even with the plans you have in place for the future of your children, it is God who will ensure that all goes well with you and with your children after you. On our way to the mortuary, someone in the car pointed to a house she rented and lived in for thirteen years, but which is now in the bush. The owner died and though she had children, the family has been arguing over whose house it should be. Now, with all the witchcraft involved, no one can live in that house. If you have the Lord as your Master and King, your future is secured. Your life and the lives of your descendants will be taken care of. That is a reason to celebrate God and His loving commitment to build you and yours, in Jesus' Name.

God of Possibilities

YOUR GOD SHALL PROVIDE FOR YOU!

The greatest fear of new beginnings is the provision of resources. I have met many people who started off with their parents not being able to get them past elementary school, but God got them to the highest levels of their education. Some now include doctorate holders, university professors, and senior statesmen or women. Chatting with one such person recently, he told me how he went to elementary school without shoes. His mother would even punish him for trying to help others with the little food she had for him. Today, he is helping many people because he is reasonably wealthy. God can provide!

Another person managed with parental help to go through secondary school but could not go further. He then started as a night watch person in an institution, saved money from it and got into university, then teacher's training and eventually got a doctorate. The start was rough, but with God all things are possible.

A widow came to Elisha and told him that her husband had died. Her debtor was on her neck to pay the debt which she could not pay. Elisha asked what she had. She had only a little quantity of olive oil.

"Elisha said, 'Go around and ask all your neighbors for empty jars. Don't ask for just a few. Then go inside and shut the door behind you and your sons. Pour oil into all the jars, and as each is filled, put it to one side'" (2 Kings 4:3-4 NIV).

With her two sons the widow got all the jars they could. They shut the door behind them and started pouring the "little oil" into the jars. **"When all the jars were full, she said to her son, 'Bring me another one.' But he replied, 'There is not a jar left.' Then the oil stopped flowing" (2 Kings 4:6 NIV).** Note from here:

- She approached the prophet. You should reach out to God with your need. Learn to pray. Thank God you can pray to God, but you can also go to someone, whom God lays in your heart, who can give you good counsel.
- God used the little she had. Whatever little you have, put it into use. Invest it and remember that God says we should not ignore little beginnings. God will bless your efforts with great results.
- Obey divine directives, no matter how foolish they may be. Just obey. Remember the Bible says the foolishness of God is greater than man's wisdom. Just trust Him.
- They shut the door behind them. Do not make much noise about what God is doing for you. Just be calm, resilient and let the results speak for you as God blesses.

- Please do your best to keep good relationships. God often uses people to meet the needs of others. The widow was able to get much oil because she and the children could freely ask for jars from the neighbors. If they had related badly, they would not have been able to get those jars.

Beloved in the Lord, as hard as life is, God still makes a way for His children. Please, do what He is laying on your heart without hesitation. The beginning may be small and uncertain, yet please, take the step and trust God for the provision. As long as you go with God, you will be blessed and be a blessing to many, in Jesus' Name.

Day 59   God of Possibilities

DARE WITH YOUR ABLE GOD!

Sometimes life is so hard that we see some situations with our eyes and immediately perceive our inability. We do not attempt solutions; yet, we have a God who is able to do immeasurably more than we think or imagine. Sometimes unless you dare, you do not attempt to conquer an impossible situation. You may not realize that the storm you face is only in the teacup or that the seeming mountain is only an anthill.

When a seventy-five-year-old man who had never been to school at all decided that he was going to read and learn to write, you can imagine the battle he had with his children and the discouragement he had in the community. Well, a few years later his name made it in national news as the oldest person to have passed the First School Leaving Certificate. He dared and conquered the reading nightmare.

One would have thought that little Vietnam would have simply surrendered to mighty USA when the US invaded them. No! They stood their ground, fought, and gave America a calamitous history that is indelible in the politics of that great nation. Do not ignore the little beginnings. Catch the spirit of it!

When David showed up from the field where he was tending his sheep, Israel was quaking with fear before a seemingly invincible giant, Goliath. David's decision to face Goliath seemed like the most stupid one ever made in the history of that nation. His brothers, warriors, were well vexed at his childish daring. The king was perplexed by his refusal to face Goliath without armor. But David dared! He explains his action in his war declaration speech to the Philistine giant: "... **'You come against me with sword and spear and javelin, but I come against you in the name of the Lord Almighty, the God of the armies of Israel, whom you have defied"** (1 Samuel 17:45 NIV). David did not go against him in his own strength. He dared to face Goliath because he knew God was with him. God did not disappoint him. The giant quickly tumbled down like a dry leaf waiting to be plucked by just a little wind.

Beloved in the Lord, what is it that you are looking at that is drying the saliva off your mouth, and you know not what to do? Is it an investment you need to make where the financing is not coming? Is it a family problem that has become an unremovable thorn in your flesh, or is it an oppressive boss you are too frightened to challenge for wrongdoing against you? The school you are afraid to attempt because it looks too expensive may just be God's avenue for a great future for you. David dared because He knew his God was with Him. He is your God! He is with you! Dare for and with Him and the God of results will give you the desired result in Jesus' Name.

When David dared, Israel was saved, and his life changed immeasurably. May the Lord quicken your heart to dare, equip you to do so, and accompany you to conquer, for His glory. Then, you will be blessed and bless others, in Jesus' Name.

LIVE IN THE REALM OF POSSIBILITIES!

So much that happens to humanity depends greatly on how much possibility we see in life. Given the complications and difficulties in life, we often see things as hardly possible, because we weigh happenings from our own abilities. God teaches us is to know the possibilities of life are not determined by us, but by Him.

I know a young faith-filled lady. Her father is so irresponsible that he has been in detention several times. Her mother is struggling with such a low-income level that taking care of all their children is horrendously pressing on her. Yet, the young girl looked me in the face and told me, "I am going to get a degree in fashion designing though no university offers that in my country." She was struggling through secondary school at the time. I shouted "Amen," hugged her and we prayed with tears in our eyes as she was telling me about her desires amidst a problem that had made her quit school and embittered her with the irresponsible parent. Well, in about a decade she walked across the graduation line in a foreign university with a degree in fashion design. Hallelujah! God can do it for you too!

Peter and his friends had seemingly concluded that the rich in their society were heaven-bound. They probably thought that when life is easy, it is easier to reach out to

God and stay with Him. They were shocked when Jesus told them:

"… 'Truly I tell you, it is hard for someone who is rich to enter the kingdom of heaven. Again I tell you, it is easier for a camel to go through the eye of a needle than for someone who is rich to enter the kingdom of God'" (Matthew 19:23-24 NIV).

The disciples were so shocked that they asked Jesus who then can be saved. His answer was perplexing: **"'… With man this is impossible, but with God all things are possible'" (Matthew 19:26 NIV).** Jesus was not telling them this to mean that the rich cannot enter heaven, but that it was only God who could make it possible for them to enter. God can do anything, but God will do only that which will give Him glory.

Beloved, yes, God has set rules and regulations on how things work in the universe, yet He also intervenes from time to time to go around a rule if that would not cause any trouble, just to let something great happen in the life of His faithful one. He stopped the earth from rotating, so the sun stood still (phenomenology) and Israel won a battle. He is the same God in whom you serve and believe Beloved of the Most High. Ask God to help you to stop looking at life from the angle of impossibility. See ill health or sickness in you or your house as curable, whatever the doctors have said. When you open your heart, God may save miraculously or lead you to some doctor you cannot now imagine. Stop pushing that dream the Spirit has been laying in your heart away with unbelief! Do not say, "It is impossible because I do not see how it can happen!" I speak possibility into your belief system, and divine intervention for its accomplishment into that project you have trusted God to accomplish for years which has not been seeming possible, in Jesus' Name.

If you want to have breakthroughs in life and accomplish great things, you must hold on to the God of impossibilities with tenacity and refuse to give up your expectation until it is accomplished. You serve an Impossibility Specialist! Hold that in your heart as you reach out to the lost, as you look at your projects for this year, and as you look at that difficulty in your life, home, village, community, or nation that has been too stubborn to go away. You cannot accomplish it but God will do it for you and you shall be blessed and bless others, in Jesus' Name.

As you move on with your life this week, challenges may come and sometimes very strong. I pray that your foot will not slip; that God will keep you from falling. Should you feel at any point that your strength is failing; your wisdom is getting short of the challenge before you; your spirituality is seeming insufficient for the temptation before you; or your wits are far below that needed for the opportunity before you; for whatever reason, and in whatever situation you feel insufficient, remember that God is the strength of your heart and your portion forever.

There is nothing He cannot do for you. Trust Him, rely on Him and be at peace in Him; and it shall be well with you. Oh, that many good things will happen to you because you are a praying person! Oh, that in the frailty of your being, God will make you a winner in life, in Jesus' Name.

Christian Life

Day 61 *Christian Life*

LET GOD PREPARE YOU!

I spent some hours with a friend from a high class in his nation. We had a good conversation. It is exceptional in his nation to have people of his background be so passionate about Jesus, so I had to find out how he got to that place. His background is a difficult one. He experienced a good life in the upper class but also lived through the pain that a life dedicated to occultism produces. By God's grace he was able to reject occultism and struggled greatly against the passions, commitments, and even the fellowship of the family. That is how he found Christ and developed the passion and knowledge that now empowers him to live his faith among the people of the upper class and stay away from any spiritual distractions.

Most of the time, God uses our background, life experience and involvement to prepare us for what He wants to do with us in His vineyard. Moses could not understand that God directed him to the desert to prepare him rather than to other nations to which he could have escaped. After forty years in the desert, he came back to Egypt, led Israel out and spent forty years leading them in that hard place. When David was taking care of his father's sheep, he could hardly know that God was training him to bring victory to

Israel, and lead Israel as king, writing much about God as the shepherd and us as the sheep. Today, David's Psalm 23 is a great encouragement to many. Can you see the depth of his experience in coining that Psalm?

"The Lord is my shepherd, I lack nothing. He makes me lie down in green pastures, he leads me beside quiet waters, he refreshes my soul. He guides me along the right paths for his name's sake. Even though I walk through the darkest valley, I will fear no evil, for you are with me; your rod and your staff, they comfort me. You prepare a table before me in the presence of my enemies. You anoint my head with oil; my cup overflows. Surely your goodness and love will follow me all the days of my life, and I will dwell in the house of the Lord forever" (Psalm 23:1-6 NIV).

Put David's shepherding life and his battles with Saul side by side and see the depths of the riches of this Psalm! Experiencing God through work and life can be quite an enriching training for service.

Beloved, Jesus prepared James, who grew up by Him, for leadership in the church. Paul was highly educated, thus ready to minister to kings and philosophers. He did so very effectively. John tells us he was the disciple whom Jesus loved. He writes about love more than any of the Bible writers.

How is God preparing you? Is He using some painful experiences like Moses experienced? Is God leading you through stressful situations like David's for thirteen years? Is God taking you through education and you are angry that you do not have jobs after that? Have you survived witches and wizards in your family and at work? What has God done in your life and how are you using that experience in your service to Him? I pray that you may be able to say like Paul, **"But by the grace of God I am what I am, and his grace to me was not without effect. No, I worked harder than all of them - yet not I, but the grace of God that was with me" (1 Corinthians 15:10 NIV).** When you recognize God's Hand in what you are and in all your experiences and allow Him to work through them, you will be a great blessing to others and be greatly blessed, in Jesus' Name.

BE PUSHFUL TO BE USEFUL!

Of my class of about sixty pupils with whom I finished primary school over forty years ago, I can remember about four without stress. While most of them concluded that they did not have money to go to secondary school and either just resigned into subsistence farming or getting married, one struggled and established a photography business. He was pushful, well known in the village, and must have been the first of the class to own a house. The other one emerged from wherever he was some twenty years after we had finished school, went to a Bible college, and has been a pastor ever since. However, I go home and meet a few others who are just happy in their quiet, "peaceful" life, not bothering to have an impact on anyone. They are storytellers in the bars and village squares. They are not pushful!

Even inheritance is not enough to make one a great and influential person. I am sure that like me, you can spot people who inherited and ended up just folding up the businesses they took over. The son of one of the first tycoons in my community was quite popular shortly after his father died. His father was popular for making the money, and the son was popular for spending it. Only a few years after the father's death, he brought the business to its knees and out of shame, he relocated to another community where he dwells so quietly that he is not only unnoticed but hardly ever mentioned, though he is alive. Another guy rented out rooms in his father's dilapidated hotel just to have money to drink to stupor. For not being pushful in his life, he could not build on his parents' success. Life is not meant for watchers and talkers but for hardworking people who refuse to take "impossible" for an answer.

The Bible is clear on this subject:

- **"Those who work their land will have abundant food, but those who chase fantasies have no sense" (Proverbs 12:11 NIV).** As children, we would "own cars" that passed by. One would say, "All the red cars are mine," and others would choose their own colors. But hardly did it go beyond that. Ah! I met someone who has a dream of owning a Rav 4 and at over fifty years of age, the person is working hard at it; and about to graduate from a school that could provide a job that would enable owning a Rav 4. Pushing for what one desires with passion is the way to success and influence.
- **"Diligent hands will rule, but laziness ends in forced labor" (Proverbs 12:24 NIV).** In my high school, it was the student in the first position in class (academically) who was class prefect. Diligence leads to hard work. The diligent person can rule administratively or as the business elite of the community, while the lazy person ends up in forced

labor because he or she cannot beg forever and must eat; thus is forced to work.
- May your testimony be like that of Paul, for whatever passion or burden God has laid in your heart: **"To this end I strenuously contend with all the energy Christ so powerfully works in me" (Colossians 1:29 NIV).** If you have Christ in you, you have the energy and wisdom needed for life. Listen to Him.

There are many obstacles and blockages in life but with some pushfulness and refusal to give up on what is right and impacting, you will be most useful to yourself, to your family, community, and to God. The Lord's grace is sufficient for you. Use it, push in it, and be successful and impactful. Then, the heaven and the earth will celebrate you, in Jesus' Name.

Day 63 — Christian Life

SACRIFICE IS NOT A WASTE!

I saw in the social media about the match bonuses or compensations that the Cameroon government planned to give to her players. Two caught my attention: a bonus for "presence" and one for "participation!" That means that by simply being in Cameroon for the competition, the player receives a compensation. Should a player play even without winning, he receives a compensation. That is so, because in coming to play at the tournament the player possibly leaves behind his family and other things of personal interest as well as his team where he plays professionally. Whenever these bonuses are not paid, the players are reluctant to come again when called. They sacrificially come when they know that their sacrifice is not a waste. In life people are happy to sacrifice when such would not be wasted.

The conversation between Jesus and the disciples, especially Peter's intervention, sounds like the apostles sacrificially left their professions and "riches," at least partly, knowing that the rich shall enter heaven. When Jesus told them that only God could make the rich enter heaven, Peter asked Jesus: **"'We have left everything to follow you! What then will there be for us?'" (Matthew 19:27 NIV).** Certainly Peter and the rest of the disciples needed some compensation after leaving their all for Jesus.

Beloved, maybe you have left much of your time and resources for the Lord but are wondering how that will be helpful to you. Or you have been hesitating in giving your life to Jesus because you do not see what you will gain. Has God been calling you to ministry or to sacrificial service but you have not responded because you do not see the good that it will bring to you?

Jesus told Peter, "**... everyone who has left houses or brothers or sisters or father or mother or wife or children or fields for my sake will receive a hundred times as much and will inherit eternal life. But many who are first will be last, and many who are last will be first**" **(Matthew 19:29-30 NIV).** Leaving is gaining! Sacrificing is sowing and there will be a reaping.

May the Lord help you, dear friend, to not just sow by giving money to prophets to pray for you. May you sow by living sacrificially for God, serving Him with your time and resources, and obeying His call upon your life for ministry in or out of the church. Whatever you do in word or deed, do it for the Lord and pay the price. You may not be able to see how it will be a blessing to you but be confident in God's faithfulness to bless. He knows the end before beginning. Go all out sacrificially; **"Cast your bread upon the waters, For you will find it after many days" (Ecclesiastes 11:1, NKJV)** and serving sacrificially for the Lord is a highway to divine blessings. Do so and be blessed and be a blessing, in Jesus' Name.

Christian Protection

Day 64   *Christian Protection*

BE NOT SHATTERED: THEY GATHER TO SCATTER!

The world is so much of a battleground that we can say as Paul said, that we face death all day long. The worst of situations is there are always people who are ready to destroy others at the slightest opportunity, especially when there is a bit of wrongdoing. Others destroy for no wrong at all. The challenge is to remain faithful and let God fight.

Both as young boys and as a community we grew up in a community together. There is this person who was noted for working against the success of someone he noted as blessed or doing something that would lead to a blessing. He was very careful and subtle. In fact, only in looking back have I realized that fact, as it was not easy to see then. Now, I remember cases in which he got individuals entangled in accusations although most of them came out blameless and harmless. As one can imagine, he ended up living an isolated life from the community.

The psalmist had experiences of facing the crowd of accusers and attackers. His experience of deliverance is an encouragement for me and for you. God was there for the writer of the Psalm! He tells us, **"When I said, 'My foot is**

slipping,' your unfailing love, Lord, supported me" (Psalm 94:18 NIV). His safety and joy was in the Lord. God turned to him when he was in danger and called for help.

Those around the Psalmist did not do same. His greatest enemy was the king. How does an individual stand in battle against a king unless the Lord is with him? The king had the army, the logistics, alliances, and all that was needed for battle, except God! The Psalmist was not shattered by the strength that faced him, as the leader lacked God, the greatest fighter. Hear the Psalmist:

"Can unjust leaders claim that God is on their side - leaders whose decrees permit injustice? They gang up against the righteous and condemn the innocent to death. But the Lord is my fortress; my God is the mighty rock where I hide" (Psalm 94:20-22 NLT).

God did not disappoint him!

Beloved in the Lord, it is not the number of those who gather against you that determines your victory, it is the greatness of the God you serve. Yours is to:

- Seek to be innocent. Let righteousness protect you and keep you close to God.
- Remain with God for your safety. Do not seek safety in alliances, fetishes or schemes that are also destructive. No! Seek safety in the Lord. Be confident that if your foot slips, the Lord will hold you up. God will fight for

you so it does not matter how much, how often, and how serious they gather against you, as they will scatter at His command.

Hold on to the Lord, because **"God will turn the sins of evil people back on them. He will destroy them for their sins. The Lord our God will destroy them"** (Psalm 94:23 NLT). You will be saved and blessed, in Jesus' Name.

Day 65   Christian Protection

BE FOCUSED NOT SURPRISED!

Some who raise cattle in the part of the world where I come from also have sheep among the cattle in their ranches. The sheep do not feel threatened. After all, cows are neither carnivorous nor violent and would not destroy the sheep unless by accident. Two animals that definitely cannot dwell together are sheep and wolves. The wolf is carnivorous and dangerously vicious. It would easily feed on sheep. After all, the sheep are weak and cannot run half as fast as the wolf. Yet, Jesus says to you and me, **"I am sending you out like sheep among wolves. Therefore be as shrewd as snakes and as innocent as doves" (Matthew 10:16 NIV).** What a reality! How can sheep survive among wolves?

Shrek was the name given to a sheep that escaped from a farm in New Zealand and lived in a cave in the wild for six years. That means that the wool was not shorn off its body during that length of time. The fact that Shrek was in a cave kept the wolves from coming after it. However, wolves once attacked the sheep but could not kill it because their teeth could not penetrate the thick, soft wool on the sheep's body. Jesus says, when we are as sheep among wolves, we should be, "as shrewd as snakes and as innocent as doves." It is God's desire that His children be as gentle and harmless as sheep. So, one piece of the fruit of the Spirit is gentleness. You may find yourself surrounded by violent, unfriendly people; some who resemble you in "visible intentions," but have dangerous hidden motives. You may notice around you, people who pretentiously give you the impression that you are friends because you work together or are in the same profession, or even come from the same family, but you see their manipulative skills against your wellbeing. How do you react? Do not be surprised and definitely do not be afraid. Be focused on you, your vision or passion and on the Lord.

Child of God, in such an environment be as clever as a snake. Snakes are always hiding; in holes; under rocks, in caves, and other places. Hide under the divine Rock, Jesus. Like Shrek, the Rock of Ages will keep you. He is the best place to hide. He will keep you from those violent attacks and preserve you for as long as He keeps you on earth. But should the wicked get at you, stay calm and be as gentle as a dove. God will fight your battles. To be gentle is to answer softly, react with emotions under control and anger not allowed beyond sunset each day. Jesus? **"He was oppressed and afflicted, yet he did not open his mouth; he was led like a lamb to the slaughter, and as a sheep before its shearers is silent, so he did not open his mouth" (Isaiah 53:7 NIV).** He never fought back because the glory of God was greater, more important than His rights! When you are led to speak up, speak to correct, not to win. Speak, not to claim your right while others and the family, village, nation, or church hurt; but speak to make things right and give God the glory. When you walk like sheep among wolves, remember, you are not alone. Jesus is with you and it will be well with you, in Jesus' Name.

Provision & Obedience

Day 66   *Provision & Obedience*

GO: HE WILL MEET YOUR NEEDS!

Even if we have someone to blame because life has become complicated it will not change the facts of our problems. Our parents had vast pieces of land in the days of their youth and needed children to cultivate them. So, they delivered many children. One of the things I miss from the village is the vastness of space. Our farmlands were large, and we still had sufficient bushes close to the village for hunting. Yes, there was hunting for bush animals that are now protected, if at all available. Today, population growth has pressured the land, pushing many out of the village and forcing both migrants and those in the village to the cities to reduce their family sizes. Life can be hard!

As young adults we looked forward to July and August, the months in which corn was harvested. It was our duty to carry the corn from the farm to the house where it was stored in barns for consumption during the rest of the year. That was hard and very tedious work, yet it was enjoyable because we often did it in groups, moving from one family farm to the other until it was done for the whole village.

There were also some women who, for one reason or the other, did not have farms or their crops did not produce well. They simply had to assist in harvesting, moving from one farm to the other. They took their baskets along with them. At the end of the day, those baskets were well filled with good-quality corn. They went home from each farm with a basket full of corn. After a few farms, they had enough to keep them for a few months at least.

Things have changed so much, though this practice is still going on in our villages. Now, little farms yield much but few people have access to land. City life is demanding and few live in affluence. But two things have not changed:

- The God who sustained and sustains in the villages is the same One who sustains in towns and cities. His love, ability, and will to provide for His people has not changed. Peoples, civilization, economies, and even politics change but God does not. He is the same yesterday, today and forever.
- God's promises still stand. What He said and did for Israel thousands of years ago is what He promises and will do for you and for me today. He told Israel, **"Your basket and your kneading trough will be blessed" (Deuteronomy 28:5 NIV).** The basket contained the fruit of grain, and the kneading trough was like the board on which they mixed flour and leaven. This was left in place to rise before being made into bread. God promised and provided for their daily needs (in the trough) and for their sustenance (in the basket).
-

Beloved, Israel's God is your God, and the promise is for you as well. Take your basket, your needs and expectations, first to the Lord and then to wherever He directs you to go! Yes, take that last food in your store or last bill or coin in your purse. Do not save it for tomorrow and die of hunger now. No! Trust God for your next meal, and trust God to meet your needs. When He does and you are blessed, be His Hands to others. Both the one who carries the basket to the corn farm and the one who owns the corn farm are blessed. Go! The unchangeable Lord, your God shall meet your needs and bless you, in Jesus' Name.

Day 67 — Provision & Obedience

LEARN TO LISTEN

I had started out on a journey but realized that because I bought some things on the way, my luggage was too small. I went into an open market and bought a big suitcase. I was just about to walk away when I realized that I did not count the money I received as change from the bank note I gave. I stopped, counted it and realized that the seller had given me too much. I turned back to give the excess balance to him. "Sir." I said to him. "You have made an error in giving me change." I was still talking when he started yelling at me and calling me names. He was very racist and provocative in his remarks. I got angry and since he did not give me a chance to speak, I took my suitcase and walked away with the money. Yes, I should still have given him the money, but he would have helped me and himself had he just listened.

God speaks, but only those who really listen can hear Him. It takes real attention to hear God. Elijah, a major prophet, was afraid of Ahab and walked a whole day to find some safety, but in that safety he complained to God. He lay down to rest and an angel of God brought him food. **"So he got up and ate and drank. Strengthened by that food, he traveled forty days and forty nights until he reached Horeb, the mountain of God"** (1 Kings 19:8 NIV). Why? To hear God. Even there, it took quite a lot of effort to get Elijah's attention so he could hear God.

"The Lord said, 'Go out and stand on the mountain in the presence of the Lord, for the Lord is about to pass by.' Then a great and powerful wind tore the mountains apart and shattered the rocks before the Lord, but the Lord was not in the wind. After the wind there was an earthquake, but the Lord was not in the earthquake. After the earthquake came a fire, but the Lord was not in the fire. And after the fire came a gentle whisper. When Elijah heard it, he pulled his cloak over his face and went out and stood at the mouth of the cave. Then a voice said to him, 'What are you doing here, Elijah?'" (1 Kings 19:11-13 NIV).

My suitcase seller could not hear me because he was selfish and suspicious. Possibly he had never had someone coming to give money back, and he was racist and did not know me. God took the prophet away from distractions to get his complete attention. Thank God today we can travel to the "mountain [presence] of God" in our bedrooms!

Beloved, the world around us is very distractive. Your mind itself can be very distracted when it is filled with fears, selfishness, suspicion and prejudice. God speaks through circumstances, through people and by His Spirit through His word. All these need attention. Unless you are "all ears" and listen to God at all times, you will miss some significant things God wants to reveal to you. Make time to be quiet before God, reading His word, talking little or not at all, except asking Him to speak to you. Do not read one verse for one minute and pray for thirty minutes. When you hear God well, your prayer may not need to be very long because you would have gotten some answers from what He said. God speaks because God wants His children informed, obedient, and guided by His truth. Learn to listen to God. Your life will be most guided, most directed, most blessed, and more of a blessing to others, in Jesus' Name.

WISDOM IS NOT ONLY LEARNED IN SCHOOL

If all the wisdom we get were learned in school I am sure that life would be quite hard. That does not mean that education is not useful, but it is not always enough. Some years ago, I drove with a brother on very bad roads leading to the village. He kept commenting on the fact that he could not drive on that road and wondered how those cars got maintained. He had been out of the country for a long time studying and had become a professor in mechanical engineering in Europe. If he was in our nation for some time, he would need to gradually learn and get used to driving on our roads again. If that car had mechanical problems, he probably would not fix it because he did not have the tools. He would take it to some local mechanic versed in solving car problems in their context. Learning is a process. School does just part of it.

Moses, we are told, was well schooled in the wisdom of Egypt. Having grown up with the pharaohs, he certainly received the best. But when God wanted to use him, God took him to the desert for forty years and trained him to know the area. He studied geography and survival, not in a class but by running after Jethro's sheep. If he could patiently lead such dull animals, he could lead stubborn Israelites. Yes, he never became a president, prime minister or even a teacher, but he was a great leader and left pages of the narratives of God's walk with Israel used to instruct generations to come.

Naaman even tried to argue out of his knowledge of rivers. He had leprosy and through the advice of his servant and the intervention of his king, the king of Aram, he found himself in Israel at the door of Prophet Elisha's house. Elisha's instruction was simple. Naaman was told to go and wash himself in the Jordan River seven times and be healed. He did not find that funny at all.

"But Naaman went away angry and said, 'I thought that he would surely come out to me and stand and call on the name of the Lord his God, wave his hand over the spot and cure me of my leprosy. Are not Abana and Pharpar, the rivers of Damascus, better than all the waters of Israel? Couldn't I wash in them and be cleansed?" So he turned and went off in a rage" (2 Kings 5:11-12, NIV).

This learned great man, commander of the army of Aram, thought he knew what the prophet needed to do. He was wrong. It took the urging of Naaman's servant for Naaman to humble himself and do what Elisha told him to do. **"So he went down and dipped himself in the Jordan seven times, as the man of God had told him, and his flesh was restored and became clean like that of a young boy" (2 Kings 5:14 NIV).**

He learned to just obey!

Beloved in the Lord, when you go through life's furnace of pain and agony, look up to God and thank Him for taking you through the university of pain. You will graduate with experience and be ready for the next level to which He is taking you. Do not be too great or too learned to hear what He is saying to you through low, uneducated people. Like someone said, even the dull and the foolish, they too have their stories. Listen to them and learn. Life could be much more meaningful, taking you closer to your fulfillment, in Jesus' Name.

Wisdom

Day 69   *Wisdom*

CHRIST IS OUR WISDOM!

Nothing is wise that does not look like Christ, though there is a "wisdom of this world" which is simply the ability to discern or have good judgement. My friend told us a story of a man who was greatly provoked in the public one day. He looked at the man who had provoked him, said nothing and simply walked away. He then said to a few people around him, "Wow, I have really changed. Can you imagine that I am the one who has walked away like that? If not for Christ in me, the old me would have dealt with that fellow." Imagine the fight that would have broken out and the wounds that would have accompanied them home! I witnessed something similar in which a person was trying to separate a fight between in-laws over really little money and went home with a broken nose. The wisdom of the world attempts to preserve personal pride. But it can only go so far and withstand it only to a certain degree. The wisdom of God sees the dignity of the person concerned, the respect of self, and the glory of God and is able to hold its peace extensively.

The main difference between the wisdom from heaven and earthly wisdom is earthly wisdom is a personal struggle to judge well; is almost purely a product of experience and yet, not easy to hold for long. Divine wisdom is a Person, characterized by purity and righteousness. It is a joy that comes from a sense of fulfillment, not from a burden. Christ is the wisdom of the righteous! God can use even a very unexpected source to display great wisdom and make great things happen.

"God chose the lowly things of this world and the despised things - and the things that are not - to nullify the things that are, so that no one may boast before him. It is because of him that you are in Christ Jesus, who has become for us wisdom from God - that is, our righteousness, holiness and redemption" (1 Corinthians 1:28-30).

Christ is our wisdom. The wise words, actions, and reactions He leads us to express from our judgment are characterized by righteousness and holiness. It leads to the salvation, spiritual and physical, of those involved in a situation.

Remember the wisdom of God is not found in the greatness of the person expressing it, but in the Christ or God in the person. That is how God can use the lowly or the despised things of the world, such as a poor person, to express His wisdom. Solomon says,

"I also saw under the sun this example of wisdom that greatly impressed me: There was once a small city with only a few people in it. And a powerful king came

against it, surrounded it and built huge siege works against it. Now there lived in that city a man poor but wise, and he saved the city by his wisdom. But nobody remembered that poor man. So I said, 'Wisdom is better than strength'" (Ecclesiastes 9:13-16a NIV).**

Dear friend:

- Look up to the Christ in you and know that with Him you are wise.
- Listen to His guidance and what you do or say in every situation will be wise.
- Evaluate the wisdom of what you say or do by seeing if it reflects Christ. Do not boast in your wisdom but in your Lord who gives wisdom and helps you express it.
- In any situation, never consider yourself as unworthy, little, unlearned, uneducated, or inexperienced to bring about a solution. You are a vessel of the Christ in you and He can use you greatly.
- Let not the might or power of the strong and many frighten you because wisdom is better than strength. Seek more to be wise than to be strong!

May the wisdom of God that dwells in you, even Christ Himself be manifest in and through you, to bring about peace and great blessing for you and for those around you and beyond, in Jesus' Name.

Day 70   Wisdom

WISDOM IS FOR DAILY USEFULNESS

I sat at the airport waiting for my next flight; unhappy that I needed to wait five hours before the time to leave. As I looked around, I saw others rushing, walking at top speed even on the moving stairs, trying to ensure that they did not miss their flight. I looked above me and saw the classy people, the "Miles & More" travelers receiving VIP treatment, making drink and food choices as they waited briefly for their flight time. Before I had time to swallow my saliva as I looked at them with some thought of "how I wish I was up there," my phone rang. The caller enquired where I was and when I gave the answer, the response was, "I connect myself to the grace of being at the airport. I hope you are having a great time." I laughed and said, "Of course!" That call delivered me from ravings of unwise comparison, fruitless envy and a thought of ungratefulness to God who fashions the life of each of us in accordance to His will.

A great benefit of wisdom is the ability to see things from God's perspective and interpret them constructively for self and others. Consequently, it is reacting or taking action that is also constructive for self as well as for others, and glorifying to God. Wise people think, consult and act. Unwise people act rashly; rushed by unanalyzed situations. They create more complicated situations in the process.

Wisdom is for our daily victorious and constructive living. Beloved in the Lord,…

"indeed, if you call out for insight and cry aloud for understanding,…then you will understand what is right and just and fair - every good path. For wisdom will enter your heart, and knowledge will be pleasant to your soul. Discretion will protect you, and understanding will guard you" (Proverbs 2:3, 9-11 NIV).

Dear friend, evaluate your wisdom by looking at the impact your actions and reactions have on you, on those around you and on the Name of God. At the end of all your learning and all your experiences or in none at all, ask God for the ability to speak, act and react to impact, not to impress; to influence and not to win arguments; to develop not to destroy; and to glorify God, not to be applauded. The wise are a daily blessing to others and to the Kingdom of God irrespective of circumstances. Be wise, be blessed, and bless in Jesus' Name.

SEEK WISDOM FOR YOUR LIFE!

As early as our primary (elementary) school days we thought "Sal" would be a great man and most likely a prolific writer. He articulated brilliantly and caught the attention of the whole school. Though some said he was using charms to perform so well, he proved that he was very intelligent. He finished primary school with flying colors and made his way to high school where his intelligence was acclaimed. But it seems life was not really kind to him. During my time in the university in Cameroon and elsewhere I had neither seen nor heard about him for over a decade. When I set eyes on him again, it was with sympathy. He moved around the streets with flies in his armpits writing more with his mouth than with the pen we had hoped he would weld. He still articulated very well but, more in off licenses and local liquor bars, than anywhere else thought to be productive. Is life that cruel?

No! Life is not so cruel though it may not be easy. The problem is that sometimes we mistake intelligence for understanding and erroneously take experience for wisdom. The world applauds intelligence; the ability to learn things and reproduce well and articulate accurately. But it is the Lord who gives understanding and the ability to grasp the meaning of the things we learn, say and do. God also grants wisdom; the ability to interpret the implications of what we know, say and do. Understanding makes us prosper and wisdom gives us life (Proverbs 19:8). Understanding transforms what we learn into productive knowledge. Divinely guided knowledge grows our experiences into incredible knowledge. What are the visible signs of understanding and wisdom? The Bible has an answer: **"Who is wise and understanding among you? Let them show it by their good life, by deeds done in the humility that comes from wisdom" (James 3:13 NIV).**

A wise person lives and promotes a good life and is humble. He or she is rash in neither words nor deeds. He or she is not distracted by a good vocabulary, articulated with mastery, but is motivated by the positive life he or she provokes in the audience and the appreciation of humble demonstration in practical living. The acquisition of understanding and wisdom demands looking to God in total surrender and a commitment to righteousness.

"To the person who pleases him, God gives wisdom, knowledge and happiness, but to the sinner he gives the task of gathering and storing up wealth to hand it over to the one who pleases God" (Ecclesiastes 2:26 NIV).

May the Lord grant you wisdom for life and impact, that you may be indeed blessed and bless others, in Jesus' Name.

EDIFY AND EXPOSE DIDACTICALLY

I was working hard to command the Boys' Brigade squad that was preparing for a Christmas play at our village church. I knew nothing of French except that our army is commanded in French. So, I managed to sneak a French word into the command, "Beaucoup, beaucoup." Well, everything else I said and did in that role was forgotten and ignored but "Beaucoup, beaucoup" became my nickname, a ridiculing one for a few years. Honestly, I do not even remember what the play was all about, but I remember my unliked nickname! Hahaha!

When my brother told me that he went to Europe as a student and they asked him if in Africa we sleep on treetops and he told them, "Yes, and our house is on top of the tallest tree;" I thought he was joking. When my own turn came to go to Europe, I realized he was more than serious. In fact, when I came to Cameroon for holiday and brought to them pictures of downtown Yaoundé, Cameroon, my European friends were embarrassed and shocked. They are not to blame because they just knew what western media told them. What you expose without didactical explanation, gives half-truths and deception and often misleads people and deters them from Christ.

Today, we see videos of pastors making people eat grass, washing women's private parts, beating people as ordination and cutting demons with cutlasses among other things. There is even one video with a priest explaining how much people can pay for various sins and be free to practice them. People share these videos with excitement and joy, then a serious narrative of the badness or falsehood of the church follows either by the same or others. In the process, in the name of "exposing falsehood" the church is given a bad name and those at the gate are scared and deterred from entering the church in fear of being misled. Some of these videos are actually acted **out?** by agents of darkness to discredit the gospel. Child of God, before you share, remember that as people living for the Lord:

- Our responsibility is to edify. **"If we live, we live for the Lord; and if we die, we die for the Lord. So, whether we live or die, we belong to the Lord…Let us therefore make every effort to do what leads to peace and to mutual edification" (Romans 14:8, 19 NIV).** That which does not edify should not come from a Christian because it has the potential of destruction or deterring people.
- Our responsibility is unto truth. Jesus was faced with falsehood but did not concentrate on it. Apostles: New Testament writers were faced with falsehood, particularly Gnosticism, but they did not spread their teachings. Rather, the apostles spent time on the truth, teaching what would enable people to identify

falsehood and flee from them. People cannot be liberated by a knowledge of falsehood because the face and content of falsehood changes. People get liberated by a knowledge of the truth. Jesus said it clearly, **"Then you will know the truth, and the truth will set you free" (John 8:32 NIV).**

The best way to expose falsehood is to teach the truth that enables people to identify what is false. Remember that falsehood appeals so much to the emotions, but wisdom guides the emotional. The reason people fall for false teachers is not because the false teachers are powerful or convincing but because the people, their victims, are ignorant of the truth. I was a university student when a Jehovah's Witness followed me one day from the school to my residence to preach to me. When he entered the room and saw my books, my study Bible and a set of commentaries on the shelf, he could not even sit still, let alone preach to me. He realized I was not just an economics student but a student of the Word. He walked away.

Beloved in the Lord, before you hit the "share" or "forward" button be sure you are not helping the enemy to destroy lives; be sure you are edifying someone and ensuring you expose with a teaching of the related truth from scripture. Build yourself up in the truth and build your audience with the same. Then we will all be protected and blessed, in Jesus' Name.

Grace and Mercy

Day 73 　　　　　　　　　　　　　　Grace & Mercy

WORSHIP THE GOD OF CONVICTION

I am glad that God did not make me a robot so He could control me by remote control in all I do. Yet, I pray God should never allow me to go beyond the bounds of His loving guidance just because I have the freedom of choice for my life. We had to take care of a young girl in an organization I led some time ago. The father had burnt all her clothes and taken everything from her, simply because she chose to be a Christian. But this young lady's heart was filled with overflowing joy. Although the father was quite wealthy and provided for them whatever they needed, she explained, she never had the joy that now filled her heart. You see, the father was not concerned about her joy and well-being but about his religiosity; even though that religiosity imprisoned him in a joyless world of bondage and hypocrisy.

God does not force people to believe Him and do His will. Even in the story of Jonah, where God is acting with a strong directive hand, the concluding message to Jonah and to us is not that God can make us do whatever He wants. The concluding message is that we should care about the well-being of others. The temperature was high, and Jonah felt quite hot. God made a plant grow and give

Jonah covering from the sun. Before Jonah's joy could fill his heart, God made the plant die quickly. Jonah was very angry.

"But the Lord said, 'You have been concerned about this plant, though you did not tend it or make it grow. It sprang up overnight and died overnight. And should I not have concern for the great city of Nineveh, in which there are more than a hundred and twenty thousand people who cannot tell their right hand from their left - and also many animals?'" (Jonah 4:10-11 NIV).

Jonah's story teaches us the foolishness of selfishness and the value of grace, concern, and love in a free world where personal interest can lead to selfishness, in spite of the fact that loving others really takes nothing much away from us.

Beloved in the Lord, God does not force us to obey Him. If He did, it seems like this world would be at its best because everyone would be doing what is right. But wait a minute, have you seen a child who is busy enjoying his or her game and the parents send him or her on an errand? When my mother or father did that to me, I went away grumbling and wearing a gloomy face all the way. Thank God they did not do it often! To do what is right without the heart committed to it is not the kind of humanity that God wants. God has given you a will; then, He has given you His word of truth and rightness, and the Holy Spirit to convict you to do that will. That is guided freedom. If like Pharaoh, you decide to remain in your own convictions away from His truth, His caution or warning would be that you do not prevent anyone from exercising a conviction to serve and worship Him.

- For your liberty to follow your heart.
- For His truth that God has given to guide you daily.
- For the satisfaction and fulfillment that there is in doing His will.
- For giving His Spirit to give and rekindle that conviction in you from time to time.
- For giving you the liberty to worship Him.

Dear friend, celebrate God for such loving care that opens your heart and mind to approach the throne of the Most High. Worship before that throne and be very blessed, in Jesus' Name.

Day 74   *Grace & Mercy*

WORSHIP THE RIGHTEOUS GOD!

The world is so corrupt that it is difficult to see someone who is truly committed to total integrity. When a community knows someone righteous and faithful, he or she is highly honored and highly respected. Three men dominated the stage of respect in our tribal community in the eighties and nineties. One was a medical academician, another an animal scientist and the third, a pastor politician. Their lives were exemplary. They were caring and spent much on the progress of their people. Oh yes, they were very highly respected and honored. For over two decades of their being in the limelight, I never heard any scandal or even a complaint about any of them, though one cannot say they were perfect. Righteousness is good and possible!

Three men, a legend tells us, were thieves in a community. To humiliate them, the community branded an "S" on each of their foreheads. It would be their mark until death. Two children of the next generation, who grew up not knowing the story, conversed. One asked the other, "What is the 'S' mark on these men's foreheads all about?" The friend answered, "I do not know but from what I have heard of them in our community, the 'S' must stand for saint." God had done a great transforming work in their lives. They had changed very much and won the admiration and honor of their community. That is how much our God of Righteousness changes those who trust Him.

Paul's testimony is outstanding and calls for a celebration of the God of Righteousness. Paul tells us, **"I am the least of the apostles and do not even deserve to be called an apostle, because I persecuted the church of God" (1 Corinthians 15:9 NIV).** If God was only a God of vengeance and not of grace, He would have expressed His wrath on Paul and destroyed or killed him. But because He is a righteous God who seeks righteousness in the innermost being and works it out, especially for all who desire it, He instead transformed Paul, who said:

"The grace of our Lord was poured out on me abundantly, along with the faith and love that are in Christ Jesus. Here is a trustworthy saying that deserves full acceptance: Christ Jesus came into the world to save sinners - of whom I am the worst. But for that very reason I was shown mercy so that in me, the worst of sinners, Christ Jesus might display his immense patience as an example for those who would believe in him and receive eternal life. Now to the king eternal, immortal, invisible, the only God, be honor and glory for ever and ever. Amen" (1 Timothy 1:14-17 NIV).

It is a common occurrence in Paul's writings that when he remembered the righteousness and grace God poured upon his life, he burst into worship and exalted this Great God of Righteousness.

Beloved, emulate (copy) Paul's attitude. If God has done some transformative work in your life, celebrate His righteousness. If He has not yet transformed your life into an "S" person, no matter how far you have gone into wickedness, turn back to Him and cry for mercy. He will hear you, He will transform you, and He will put a new song in your heart. It will be a song of joy and worship because God has transformed you into a personality of honor and self-respect. Through Christ, seek righteousness and celebrate the God who gives, and you shall be blessed and God glorified, in Jesus' Name.

PROBLEM: WHEN HONOR IS DEMANDED!

What a school head we had! When you did wrong and he wanted to punish you there was just one thing that could free you easily: address him as "Doctor" as many times as you could while pleading for mercy. The more you did so, the more likely "Dr." would waive your punishment. If in the process, however, you made the error of addressing him "Sir" you were likely to receive a number of strokes before he meted out whatever punishment he had for you. His honor was a no-compromise thing for him. It somehow defined him. That is one problem within our human race. Demanding honor is paradoxical because in reality you are actually asking for what you do not deserve.

Israel's first king, Saul, did not do what God wanted him to do. His sacrifice, rather than obedience cut him out of God's honor roll. Unfortunately, his desired human honor so much that at the time he should have been confessing and asking God for forgiveness, he was instead asking for human honor. Samuel told him that God had torn the kingdom away from his hands and given it to one more righteous than him. Saul's response is an unfortunate plea: **"Saul replied, 'I have sinned. But please honor me before the elders of my people and before Israel; come back with me, so that I may worship the Lord your God'" (1 Samuel 15:30 NIV).** When honor is demanded, wrongdoing is in view, and human respect and divine honor escape the victim, it can lead to significant depression.

Beloved citizen of the earth, God's grace and His enabling Spirit in your heart are there to make you "earn" the honor of your life. You earn it by allowing the Holy Spirit to bear fruit and enable you to bear the fruits of good works; expressed in practical love towards others. If for any reason you realize that you are losing your honor before God, repentance is best. Sacrificial giving to the church without a corresponding heart repentance could make things worse. Saul sought honor from those who could not keep him on the throne! God, not man, has both the agenda and road map of your destiny, to the life of your full joy. Live by the Spirit and truth; humble yourself in the presence of humanity. Then, you will honor and bless them and the God you serve will give you honor and blessing, in Jesus' Name.

Day 76   *Grace & Mercy*

LIVE BY HIS GRACE AND LOVE!

For decades I have signed all my emails at the end, "By His grace and love." This is because these two words are cardinal to my life. I would have no life without them.

It was my first year in high school and our discipline master came to the assembly the day various classes were supposed to choose their class prefects. He stood before us at the general assembly and called out "LA2 (lower sixth arts class, series 2), where is that guy from BCGE, come out." I came out and he looked at me and told me, "You are the class prefect of your class." Apparently, the school administration had had a problem with students who came from Bui College of General Education (BCGE), where I did my secondary school and concluded that BCGE students were stubborn. They believed the way to keep me in check was to make me class prefect. Haha! Whether he succeeded is another story but that was the only time I was ever an active prefect in school.

My position lasted from September to December (one term), because the rule in the school was to get the brightest student in each class as class prefect. All through my primary, secondary, high school and university in Cameroon, I was never the best student in class, even once. I only enjoyed that privilege in my university studies in Scotland and Nigeria. I know I do not live by any great wisdom. I even remember the day I wrote a Pacesetter with great excitement and got this reply from a reader, "Dr. Nfor, I wanted to send out your devotional because it is good, but I discovered that it has a lot of errors in it." I was not surprised because I make many grammatical and spelling errors and have made many errors in my life. Were man to live by the product of his excellence, I would have been long gone!

What surprises me is that I have had a positive impact in a few lives. Some people have smiled from my few words, eaten from my meager earnings, loved from my efforts at the pulpit, and in some way benefited from the mere fact of my existence. How? By the grace and love of God!

I deserve nothing. One pastor told me, "You have served long and deserve to have what you want!" No! Grace never gets deserving. There are many things I want but do not have. I accept what I have or do not have, and I am at peace because I live by grace and love from God.

I have been *wrongly* insulted from the pulpit in perfect big English grammar, castigated on social media, grieved by family, and made to look really stupid in meetings. My reply has been to smile and tell myself, "What is new about the fact that I deserve nothing positive? If I do get a little pat on the back, I rejoice; if an insult, I smile at Christ whose grace and love enables me to reach out in spite of all my shortcomings. Those who help me see my weaknesses have a right to their opinions. Even if it is rude to point them out in public and even if they are mistaken, I have a right to my life." All I ensure is that I remind myself of God's grace and love for me.

Beloved in the Lord, when you live by grace and love, no one tramples on your pride, because you have nothing to be proud of. The Bible asks a very salient question, **"For who makes you different from anyone else? What do you have that you did not receive? And if you did receive it, why do you boast as though you did not" (1 Corinthians 4:7 NIV).** You see, you are a product of divine grace and are sustained by divine love.

If you live by grace and love, you do not harm yourself because people do not love you. No! You are renewed in energy and move on when you accept and do not get people's love, because you know that God loves you.

If you live by grace and love, you are not excited and made great by what you have: including titles, degrees, and money, or by who you are: director, minister, chairman, pastor, or president, among others! No! Living by grace and love means accepting God's leading and how He uses you to do great things for humanity whom you love. *You will be known for how you impact people.* That is my desire for myself and my prayer for you because that is the best way to bless and be blessed, in Jesus' Name.

HIS GRACE IS ABUNDANT

Never give up on anyone in life. Never feel bad when the one you thought was too bad suddenly shows up as the best. Grace is God's supremacy in the choice of life's path for undeserving humanity. Yet, grace is not to be abused. When I heard that "Yusa" had become a pastor, I was surprised for a while. Yusa was dismissed from his school in our days for very bad behavior. How could he become a pastor? When did he change? What kind of pastor would he be? These questions confused me for a while before I came to my senses and thanked God for His grace. I understood grace when I saw myself teaching people with whom I had been to school in the same class; especially since I was not an A grade student in my school days with them. The formula for grace is God's love and supreme choice.

If not for grace and humility, John and the other apostles would have been angry with God for bringing Paul into the ministry. Not only was Paul absent from among the twelve apostles with Jesus; he persecuted the church. He brought havoc to the work of the apostles. In His grace, God saved Paul, and he became a great apostle. He did more work than any of the others and wrote more, thus, bringing more to the church than the other apostles. By allowing Paul to take the path he took in life, God gave him a testimony that no one else had, and which would become a very important element in Paul's understanding and teaching on grace.

Dear friend, you may think you have gone too far from the Lord to be accepted again. No! God saved Ravi Zacharias from suicide and made him a world-class defender of the gospel. God can do the same today. Is there someone you need to talk to about Jesus Christ and his or her need to be saved? Do not hesitate. Is the person too bad? Not above grace,

"For the grace of God has appeared that offers salvation to all people. It teaches us to say 'No' to ungodliness and worldly passions, and to live self-controlled, upright, and godly lives in this present age" (Titus 2:11-12 NIV).

To appropriate this gift as abundant grace, give your life to Jesus. Grace will sustain you as you allow the Holy Spirit to live in and through you daily. We are saved by grace, and we live by grace. By grace, we shall overcome the world, and by grace, we shall enter eternity. Please, be there, in Jesus' Name.

Fellowship

Day 78

HAVE A GREAT FELLOWSHIP

Ah! Food and friendship! A common phrase we used in our relationships as children was, "Chop broke pot." The expression was used for children who ate so furiously that sometimes it led to a fight over the food, resulting in the breaking of the earthen pot from which they ate. More importantly, we used the phrase as a mockery for overfeeding or eating as if one had been hungry for a long time. One of my greatest memories about food in the days of our youth, however, is the fellowship we shared around it. Sometimes as many as fifteen of us went hunting, caught a squirrel, gave the essential parts to the one who saw the animal first, the one who caught it, and the one who saw him catch it. We roasted the rest and made sure everyone ate a piece, before going back home to eat our mothers' food. Then all of us moved from one house to the next together. What great fellowship!

Today I still see food as a major thing that brings people of all classes and ages together. I have spent hours on the line on Cameroon's National Day (May 20th) for example, trying to get to dinner at the Presidency, at the Governor's Residence and that of the sub-divisional officer, to dine and chat with the great minds and servants of the nation. Food and fellowship! What treasure!

Jesus uses the analogy of food to make Himself available for a great fellowship with you. He requests, **"Here I am! I stand at the door and knock. If anyone hears my voice and opens the door, I will come in and eat with that person, and they with me" (Revelation 3:20 NIV).** Jesus, the King of all the earth, the Creator and Sustainer of the universe, the most powerful and most loving Being you can ever think of, invites you into fellowship with Him. Hallelujah! He wants to come into your space in life and have a relationship with you. He so respects your privacy and personal choice that He stands at the door of your heart, at the entrance to your will, desiring to come In and have fellowship with you. He loves you and wants to make your life so much better.

Beloved:

- If you have never opened your will to His presence, please do. Let Him into your world and give Him the chance to contribute to the greatness of your life. You will never regret it. Just accept His desire for your friendship. Ask Him to come into your heart, guide you and make His home there and your life will be so much greater.
- If you have Him in your life, enjoy His presence. Remember that He is there with you in hard times and in good times, to contribute to your best, to fight for you

for your best, and to hunt with you for the sweetest in your life and in the lives of those for whom you are responsible.

There is no greater blessing than friendship with the Greatest, fellowship with the Most Loving, and alliance with the Most Powerful, *God*! Enjoy great fellowship with Him and in your fellowship bless others too, in Jesus' Name.

Day 79 — Fellowship

RELATIONSHIPS ARE BUILT, NOT PICKED!

It looked sweet, strong, promising, and even well built, but my young friends' relationship did not last. Apparently, they had related for less than a year and believed they were God's gift for each other. They did not realize that good and fruitful relationships are cultivated, not picked. If my parents were in any trouble, we the children did not doubt who to reach out to first. Their friends were not only well known to us but also influenced our own relationships. It was and is natural that their son and I have kept close in our generation. Friendships that can back you up are not casual, not handled flippantly, and are not taken for granted. They are built over time.

Apart from his colleagues with whom Paul did ministry including Barnabas, Timothy, Titus, and Junia among others, Paul also had some wonderful friends who had a great impact on his life and ministry. He said to the church in Rome, **"Greet Priscilla and Aquila, my co-workers in Christ Jesus. They risked their lives for me. Not only I but all the churches of the Gentiles are grateful to them" (Romans 16:3-4 NIV).** This good relationship did not come by accident or by divine revelation. No! It was built over time.

"After this, Paul left Athens and went to Corinth. There he met a Jew named Aquila, a native of Pontus, who

had recently come from Italy with his wife Priscilla, because Claudius had ordered all Jews to leave Rome. Paul went to see them, and because he was a tentmaker as they were, he stayed and worked with them" (Acts 18:1-3 NIV).

They worked together, lived together and became both friends and ministry partners. We can add Lydia to the social capital that made a great difference in Paul's life and ministry.

Beloved in the Lord, life and ministry go beyond your marriage and home. Build a strong relationship within the family but stretch out! After all, the church is neither your local congregation nor your denomination. It is all those who are saved by Christ the world over. Develop meaningful relationships across congregations, out of your denomination, within the Church of God and out of the church, in your place of work or your community of residence.

Beloved in the Lord, if you find yourself without friends:

- Pride could be your problem. You are not humble enough to relate well.
- "Holier than Thou" could also be the cause. You do not relate because everyone around you is bad. But you want them to come to your rescue at your time of need!

- You are afraid or lack self-confidence. You fear that they may know your weaknesses, or you think you have nothing to offer them. No!

Christ can enable you to do all things including building meaningful relationships. Do not wait for God to give you friends. Watch for the people God brings your way. Invest in their lives and keep them close to your heart. They just may be God's hands and feet through whom God will make a great difference in your life. Cultivate fruitful relationships and be blessed even as you also bless them, in Jesus' Name.

Relationships

SOCIAL RELATIONSHIPS: BETWEEN NUMBERS & QUALITY!

How many good relationships should one attempt to have? As always, even in social relationships, quality is more important than quantity. We were waiting in a security checkpoint line for about twenty minutes to determine who was going to be admitted to the Prayer Breakfast. The senator from North Carolina was standing close to me. I greeted him, we got into a conversation and talked right up to the security post. To my great embarrassment, I put my hand into my pocket and realized that I had forgotten my passport in my hotel room which was a distance away. You can imagine what security strictness there is to a meeting in the presence of the president of the United States of America. Just one police officer's decision would have been needed to send me back for it. Thankfully my twenty-minute-old friendship with the senator saved me. I did not talk to the police. I told the senator I had forgotten my passport. He simply said to the police officer, "This is my friend from Cameroon. Sorry, he forgot his passport in the hotel room." I got through! Quality relationships can make a big difference.

Jesus was quite strategic in developing relationships. He had the groups of disciples; seventy-two, twelve and then three. From the three he chose a leader. Besides these He had a quiet relationship with others, mainly women, who came along and supported them in the ministry materially. He also related with others like Zaccheus as needs arose. He must have ministered to Joseph of Arimathea as he was willing and quick to give Him his grave.

Beloved in the Lord, there is a time and occasion for many good relationships. **"Plans fail for lack of counsel, but with many advisers, they succeed" (Proverbs 15:22 NIV).** Also, there is time for just a few but able and qualitative relationships.

"There was once a small city with only a few people in it. And a powerful king came against it, surrounded it and built huge siege works against it. Now there lived in that city a man poor but wise, and he saved the city by his wisdom. But nobody remembered that poor man" (Ecclesiastes 9:14-15 NIV).

That he was not remembered does not reduce the quality of his deed for the city. You may be that type of person!

May the Lord grant you discernment for the many and the qualitative few. Yet, remember that there is no friend who can match Jesus. Without Him, both your many and your able few could end up being a big disappointment. The most qualitative relationship is with Jesus. Do not ignore or play with it. With the many and the able few, may the Lord make your social life blessed and a blessing, in Jesus' Name.

Day 81 *Relationships*

CELEBRATE THE GOD OF RELATIONSHIPS!

What would life be like if we were made to live on this planet Earth in isolation from each other? The story of "Lord of the Flies" by William Golding is meant to give the simple answer: impossible!

Which of my friends should I talk about now? Nshandze and Nsame with whom I played as kids daily? Leonard and others with whom I went hunting as teenagers? Should I talk of my Mom with whom I worked on the farm for years, or Regina with whom I made a forty-five minute trek to school every school day for five years? Maybe I should mention Mariana as we met and walked to and from school. She became a bench mate and good friend in secondary school. Should I talk of Jeanne whose beautiful face I remember well, but who left us in tears as we buried her two weeks to the start of our GCE Ordinary Level exams. She was my bench mate that year. Should I talk of Ndzenyuy, Christopher, Lilian, and the rest of those with whom I spent beautiful weekends? Ah! How can I forget my high school mate, Tanyu, or our high school closely knit friends, Julius and Anthony? Jim Struthers had so much impact on me that I had to name a child after him. Then there are Pengsum (Chinese), Karen Garrison, John Lang, John Roise, and Sherry Carson! I cannot forget George who once was my twin brother though of different mothers. The list is long, and I will be leaving out my present close friends! Relationships are truly a blessing from God!

Of all I have listed above, a few are dead, and some I have not heard from for many years and do not even know where they are, or if they are still alive. Others, I communicate with occasionally; in Cameroon English I would say I communicate with them "one-one time." Relationships move on. Friends come and go. Some make life great, some make life miserable, and others leave scars on your life that keep teaching you each day you see them. Relationships!

There are two I have not named above. The one is my bedmate, soul mate and companion in life's journey. Of her, wise King Solomon prayed, **"May your fountain be blessed, and may you rejoice in the wife of your youth. A loving doe, a graceful deer - may her breasts satisfy you always, may you ever be intoxicated with her love" (Proverbs 5:18-19a NIV).** Yeah! We have been indeed blessed over the years! Relationships!

The second I did not name has a special place in my life. I was dirty and full of sin. In the dirt I made foolish decisions for some of the great relationships I had and cheaply sold some other relationships off despite the greatness of their value to me. Ah! I hung onto some friends who helped me walk the path of darkness and I was headed for a life of gloom and doom. Then this friend came in, cleansed me, guided me, disciplined me, helped me to have meaning in life and be sure where I am headed. Above all, this friend has never gone on holiday from me, been sick for me to take care of, never abandoned, betrayed or slandered me as some have found pleasure in doing, and above all, He gave His life to death on the cross that I may be free and live. Free I am, Hallelujah! Truly, **"One who has unreliable friends soon comes to ruin, but there is a friend who sticks closer than a brother" (Proverbs 18:24 NIV).** That friend is Jesus Christ.

If you do not have Him, dear friend, you have not started having the pedigree of friendship. Accept that you are a sinner because you sin. Believe He died for you because He did. Confess your sins with repentance because He is ready to forgive you, then ask Him to come into your heart and take control of your life. Depend on His friendship daily because He will never disappoint you. If you do this or already have Jesus as your friend, celebrate God for the gift of friendship and for establishing relationships. Bless Him for blessing you through relationships and ask Him to help you be a blessing to others in all your relationships. You will indeed be blessed, in Jesus' Name.

Day 82   *Relationships*

CONFRONT YOUR PROGRESS BLOCKERS!

In this strange world, even loving, consciously or unconsciously, sometimes constitutes progress blockages, if not progress haters. It was a pathetic reality when a mother visited her son, whose business was thriving, and brought chaos into the family. She would not allow the man's wife to have a say in the house or in the business, arguing that it was her son's toil, although his wife was a career woman who brought home her own income. Months after the start of this strange battle, the man was divorced, the business shrank, and the mother went back home. How could a mother become the enemy of her own son's progress?

Imagine what a great ally David would have had in his friend Jonathan, were it not for Jonathan's father who hated David passionately and kept his son Jonathan by his side. In reality, Saul delayed the progress of Israel and blocked whatever God would have done for his son Jonathan, had Jonathan worked with David in the progress of the nation. Unfortunately, Jonathan was more committed to his father (or family) than to truth, rightness and the one he really loved, David. At last, Jonathan died with his father in a battle against his friend David. What killed Jonathan? It was his father's disobedience to God, Saul's hatred for anointed David and Jonathan's inability to see that he could refuse being involved in a fight against the Lord's anointed. If only he had discerned well!

Beloved in the Lord, God has given you family and friends for your social fulfillment and progress. When those who should promote your progress start to block it, look beyond them to the Father who loves you completely and has a great plan for your progress. After all, He is most powerful and does not lose a battle. Paul faced all kinds of blockages in his life. Two of his confessions illuminate as you face this strange world of the persistent battle to progress. Paul tells the Romans:

"... To their own master, servants stand or fall. And they will stand, for the Lord is able to make them stand" (Romans 14:4 NIV). When you make the Lord your master, He will be able to make you stand, and no one or nothing will pull you down.

Again, Paul confessed to Timothy: **"The Lord will rescue me from every evil attack and will bring me safely to his heavenly kingdom. To him be glory for ever and ever. Amen" (2 Timothy 4:18 NIV).** Make the Lord your commander and your fighter, and it will be well with you. He will take care of your visible and invisible battles. He will take care of the blockages that are in your way, and surely, the Lord will get you to that wonderful plan that He has for your life.

The Lord will fight for you, friend. Stand with Him and stay with Him as your greatest ally and master of all. Trust Him for a victorious battle for your future, in Jesus' Name.

GIVING

GIVING IS AN IMPACTFUL INVESTMENT!

Can you remember the greatest gifts you ever received, from whoever, whenever? I know a few but will talk about two. My mother had many brothers and sisters. I am not even sure how many of them there were. Two stood out for me, especially in my high school and university days. Once, when I was leaving for school, one of those uncles gave me a piece of soap to wash my clothes. That remained in my heart and seriously motivated my connection to him. While I was studying outside of the country, one recorded music on a tape and sent it to me. This absolutely drew us together such that I was so happy to take care of his responsibilities when he was not there anymore. Although it was just a tape, it moved me to do things for him later in life worth more than a thousand tapes. Simple gifts can go a long way to create impact, bring change, and lead to a great life and love relationship thereafter. Do not hesitate to stretch out your hand to give. Never see what God lays in your heart to help someone with as small.

Remember Tabitha. She lived in a place called Joppa. She loved and was generous, especially towards the poor. She died, and they cleaned her body and put it in a room. Then, they called Peter who came and entered the house where they lay her body.

"Peter sent them all out of the room; then he got down on his knees and prayed. Turning toward the dead woman, he said, 'Tabitha, get up.' She opened her eyes, and seeing Peter she sat up. He took her by the hand and helped her to her feet. Then he called for the believers, especially the widows, and presented her to them alive" (Acts 9:40-41 NIV).

Her giving touched lives such that the people would not want her to die, and God added her years on earth. Giving is a great, impactful investment.

Beloved in the Lord, do people know you for what you have or for what you do with what you have? If you die today, would people mourn for all your property left to rot, or for the impact you had upon their lives? **"A gift opens the way and ushers the giver into the presence of the great" (Proverbs 18:16 NIV).** May your giving open the way and usher you into the presence of the Great God, and you will be blessed as you bless others, in Jesus' Name.

Day 84   Giving

SELFLESSLY INSIST ON DOING WHAT IS RIGHT!

In our world of self and gain, it is easy to give up on what is right for personal comfort. This is especially true when others are happy with the decision. You can surely remember an experience most people go through as children. My father would be going out and I would insist on going with him. Sometimes my crying was not convincing, and Daddy succeeded in getting me to stay back home. But at times I insisted with all seriousness and eventually, Dad would take me along and I would be so happy. The insistence of the child to move with the Father (or mother) may be selfish, but as an adult, a selfless insisting on doing what is right can pay off greatly.

Naomi was a woman of pain. She married a Moabite but lost her husband and her two sons. So, she decided that her daughters-in-law, Orpah and Ruth should leave her. After all, she was already elderly and could not give birth again for sons to remarry the ladies. Oprah and Ruth could marry again if they left her, she argued. Besides, she decided to leave Moab and go back home in Judah. Because she insisted, Orpah decided to leave her. Ruth insisted that her entrance into Naomi's family was permanent, and she would stay with Naomi and go back home to Naomi's God and her people. At last, Naomi gave in, Ruth remained by her side and went to Judah with her mother-in-law. Finally, Ruth remarried in the family to Boaz, a relative of Naomi.

"So Boaz took Ruth, and she became his wife. And he went in to her, and the Lord enabled her to conceive, and she gave birth to a son. Then the women said to Naomi, 'Blessed is the Lord who has not left you without a redeemer (grandson, as heir) today, and may his name become famous in Israel. May he also be to you one who restores life and sustains your old age; for your daughter-in-law, who loves you and is better to you than seven sons, has given birth to him'" (Ruth 4:13-15 AMP).

In getting married:

- Ruth maintained Elimelek's family line. She also brought joy to Naomi by giving birth to a son who would eventually take care of both of them. Selflessness is a great way to eventually bring joy to others. God blesses it greatly!
- Ruth gained such admiration that she was seen as more valuable to Naomi than seven sons. Yes! Her commitment to what she believed was right: staying with her mother-in-law rather than thinking about remarrying paved the way to her remarrying for a better cause than she could have had in Moab. Now, though a woman, she is considered as being of great value to Naomi. Selflessness often uplifts in due time. Jesus selflessly gave Himself for us and was lifted to the Right Hand of His Father.

- Above all, Ruth ends up in the line of David. Her son, Obed became grandfather of David. Ruth finds herself in the family line of Jesus. When you insist on a selfless right thing, you can end up with an impact far beyond your time and imagination.

Beloved in the Lord, it is hard to be a people-blessing person if you seek personal comfort, satisfy the sentiments of others and easily give up a sacrificial right thing, even if what you do (like Orpah leaving Naomi) is not wrong as such. Child of God, be not comfortable with, "I am not wrong" but rather be moved by your conviction of what is right and helpful to others. It is a highway to blessing. May God use your insistence on selfless rightness and bless you and others far beyond your imagination and time, in Jesus' Name.

Day 85 *Giving*

BUILD AND BE BUILT!

Since the fall of Adam and Eve, it has become necessary for every human being to grow, to think better, become better in character, and eventually more productive in life. That process takes place in a world where Satan is active in making people bad but also in a world where the Spirit of God has gifted people for the good of one another. I wonder what I would have become had I not had good friends as a child in secondary and high school and as an adult!

Yes, I remember my childhood friends abandoning me when I fell from a tree and wounded myself badly, but I also remember them playing with me, studying with me, and singing with me. I remember the day we were on a trip from our rice farming part of the village and I was carrying a bag of pears. When it got too heavy for me and I started crying, one of them took some from my bag and added them to his while I carried those I could. I received the rest back from him when we got home. Ah! It would be silly for me to attempt to look for an example of such assistance I have had as an adult. That would fill volumes!

When I think of what people have done for me to bring me where I am, I can only conclude that indeed, I have a debt to humanity that I can never finish paying. The Bible tells us, **"Let no debt remain outstanding, except the continuing debt to love one another, for whoever loves**

others has fulfilled the law" (Romans 13:8 NIV). Love means seeking the best for the other person or people at any cost, without expecting anything in return. Love gives. Love builds. Love has a boomerang effect. The more love you give, the more you receive. Loving means reaching out to build others up and in turn being built up.

More so, there is no one on earth who lacks the ability to build others up. God has given us various gifts, be they talents (for the unbeliever) or spiritual gifts (for the believer). Some people can sing enough to make you laugh when you are depressed. Others write beautifully enough to captivate your learning. Some play beautiful football to make you relaxed when watching, especially when you are tense. Others have the ability to see what is wrong with your body and tell you what to do to get well. **"Now to each one the manifestation [gifts] of the Spirit is given for the common good" (1 Corinthians 12:7 NIV).** Note the purpose: gifts are given for the common good; the good of all.

Beloved in the love and grace of God, how has God gifted you? How are you using it to build the lives of those around you for people in your circle of influence? Build and be built. That is the route to the greatest of blessings. May the Lord bless you to become more like Christ and get the best in life as you build others, in Jesus' Name.

Day 86   Giving

VALUE-GIVING BEYOND TODAY!

I always remember the first significant gift I received was a wristwatch a relative gave me about 1979. Though the man left this world, he remains in my mind. That gesture made him a friend though he never gave me anything else after that. Another gift I remember was a cassette containing recorded music. I was studying out of the country in those days when there was no internet. When I got this gift, it so connected me to home that I developed a deep love for the uncle who offered me the cassette. When he and his wife passed away, I was happy to assume responsibility for their children the best I could. It is amazing what a gift can do!

"Giving Tuesday," is a tradition established in 2012 to give an opportunity for companies to offer something specifically to charitable organizations. After Thanksgiving Day, there is super spending in the U.S. on Black Friday (the day after Thanksgiving), because many companies reduce the prices of their products that day. The idea of Giving Tuesday was instituted to enable people to do good. In 2019, Giving Tuesday raised $1.9 billion U.S. dollars in the United States of America alone. In 2022 the focus was to raise money for the war in Ukraine. Giving is a great thing but what if giving was not just a program for a day in a year but a lifestyle that makes a difference in the lives of people around you.

Beloved in the Lord, no matter how much you do not have, look around your house and see how much there is, including clothes, shoes, and dishes that you do not even use! You struggle indeed but just think about how much you use in a week to buy things that are not important to your health or life: maybe ground nuts, sweets or candies. You actually have more than you think you do. However, giving is not for those who have but for those who care enough to make a difference. What Paul said to the Christians at Ephesus is still absolutely true today: **"In everything I did, I showed you that by this kind of hard work we must help the weak, remembering the words the Lord Jesus himself said: 'It is more blessed to give than to receive'" (Acts 20:35 NIV).**

Therefore:

When you work hard and are blessed, do not look at how hard you have worked and refuse to give, even to someone you see as lazy, but God moves you to give to them. Look at your blessings and remember that you are blessed by grace and your gift could change the person's life.

- Give to help the weak. Giving among equals, especially the well-to-do, is common and rampant but the most valuable and most meaningful gifts are those that make a difference in people's lives. I remember a brother in town who, a few years ago, sent money to the elderly pastors in some villages for Christmas. Knowing what those pastors go through, I know what joy he planted in those families that Christmas season. Look around you, in your family, office, tribal meetings, church, and neighborhood. You will find someone whose life you can touch today with a simple gift of a little money (why not much if you have it), with things from your closet, your time of service or a word of encouragement.

- Beyond the single act of giving today, train your heart and mind to know you are more blessed to give than receive. Giving puts great joy in your heart, especially when you see the effects. It transforms lives and causes those affected to appreciate you, be there for you and pray for you. Giving attracts God's attention towards you as it did for Cornelius (Acts 10). Giving can open doors for you to great men and women. Besides, selfish people are never satisfied!

Dear friend, God loved us and gave us His Son for our salvation. He asked us to give even to our enemies! With love in your heart for God and for mankind; with an expectation that as Jesus promised, God will bless you when you give; practice giving as a lifestyle. Start small; start today and make a difference in someone's life and in God's Kingdom. The author of Luke says it well: **"Give, and it will be given to you. A good measure, pressed down, shaken together and running over, will be poured into your lap. For with the measure you use, it will be measured to you;" (Luke 6:38 NIV)** in Jesus' Name.

Pride and Humility

Day 87　　　　　　　　　　　　　　Pride & Humility

IN HUMILITY YOU CAN LISTEN!

Dani Osvaldo was a good footballer, but he had a history of clashing with teammates and management. This was because he thought he was bigger and better than the team. He had suspensions and transfers to various teams before settling with a much lower team, Boca Junior in Argentina. Pride and arrogance block hearing and can keep someone from becoming the best he or she can be. To hear God or the people around you, you must be humble enough to listen.

Giant Goliath must have heard of the God of Israel. When David stood before him, the proud Philistine fighter who saw himself as invincible did not hear what David was saying. David had to convince Saul of the presence and activity of God in his life before Saul could allow him to fight Goliath. Now, before the human giant, **"David said to the Philistine, 'You come against me with sword and spear and javelin, but I come against you in the name of the Lord Almighty, the God of the armies of Israel, whom you have defied'" (1 Samuel 17:45 NIV)**. The proud giant did not hear David, he only saw his smallness and responded to it.

"He looked David over and saw that he was little more than a boy, glowing with health and handsome, and he despised him. He said to David, 'Am I a dog, that you come at me with sticks?' And the Philistine cursed David by his gods. 'Come here,' he said, 'and I'll give your flesh to the birds and the wild animals!'" (1 Samuel 17:42-44 NIV).

For failure to listen, it was the flesh of Giant Goliath that ended up feeding the birds. Indeed, pride comes before a fall.

Beloved in the Lord, God has given you everything you are or have, even if that is making you proud. If you can just acknowledge God's goodness to you rather than celebrate yourself more, you will greatly commune with God and hear what He says to you. Remember Paul's admonition: **"So, if you think you are standing firm, be careful that you don't fall!" (1 Corinthians 10:12 NIV).** Part of being careful is listening to God and doing just as He says. There is no safer path in life than the life of obedience. There is no way to obey unless you hear God's command. It is impossible to hear when you do not listen. It is hard to listen when you are too proud to see your need. In humility, let God speak to you daily and you will be led in a victorious procession throughout your life, in Jesus' Name.

Day 88   Pride & Humility

HARD TIMES CAN BE TREASURE TIMES TOO!

I had just gotten back from university studies (all done in English) with a master's degree when I got an opportunity to write. My senior gave me the responsibility to report on a conference we were hosting. I had written for the church monthly newspaper for four years, did some poetry, and thought I had some writing skills although I knew my spelling was an abysmal part of my writing skills, and still is. I got the shock of my academic life two days after I submitted the handwritten report. It came back to me with almost every sentence underlined for problems of grammar, spelling, syntax, or misplaced facts. I was pretty angry. Yes, I realized that my "daddy" who edited the scripts wanted me to know that coming from a university abroad did not mean I was more intelligent than him, and we had interesting discussions. I took the time after my frustrations died down, and went through the red-painted scripts, did all the corrections I could, explained those I did not think needed correction, and resubmitted. This tough moment taught me humility, how to deal with criticisms, and improved my writing skills. For one thing, I learned to keep writing without any emotional bias. Dark moments can be treasured moments.

Israel knew dark moments and hard times in their history. Even when Jesus was born the Savior of the world, instead of the news of His birth bringing peace and tranquility to

Israel, it brought hatred that ended with the nation being wiped off the world map for over eighteen hundred years. Only history could tell someone that the present vibrant, well respected and highly developed Israel ceased to be a nation for that length of time in history. Prophet Isaiah had said centuries before,

"I will go before you and will level the mountains; I will break down gates of bronze and cut through bars of iron. I will give you hidden treasures, riches stored in secret places, so that you may know that I am the Lord, the God of Israel, who summons you by name" (Isaiah 45:2-3 NIV).

God can make hard times treasurable. When it is tough:

- Trust God's leading. He has promised to go before you. God is always going before us because He is the God of yesterday, today, and tomorrow. He knows what you go through before you get there. He sets the plans in place before you get there. Trust His leading.
- Trust God's victory. He has promised to level the mountains and cut off all gates. No matter what stands before you: powerful, numerous wicked people, tough administration, frightful exams, a hideous journey, a hard-hearted jury or whatever, trust God to deal with it and help you overcome.
- Trust God to bless you with it. God has treasures for you in those dark places. God never leads His children through situations that do not end up blessing them.

No matter how horrible it looks, trust God to bless you in it. He will show you the blessings at the fulness of time.
- Remember He loves you. This is not the only text in which God talks of summoning or knowing you "by name." This indicates His love and concern for the human being, for you as His own. You are precious in His sight, and He has you at heart, even when the waves of life are battering you. He may seem to be watching but is neither laughing nor ignoring you. God stands with you to see you through.

Child of God, whatever troubles you face now or tomorrow, remember that some of your greatest treasures are hidden there. May God enrich you through your dark moments and cause you to enrich others with those treasures, in Jesus' Name.

Praise and Celebration

Day 89   *Praise & Celebration*

LET THE MUSIC PLAY ON!

Who is your favorite musician? Why? Music is so crucial to life that one cannot ignore it. Encouraging those involved in that ministry is an important assignment for everyone. My heart goes to out to young musicians around me: Tony, Frank, and Mac; my prayers go to music promoters like Bob and Rogers. My heart goes out to those struggling with their musical talents but not sure what impact they want to make with their music. Oh, that God would guide them to recognize that music is a calling and check its content to glorify God and bless humanity beyond the exercise of dancing.

I saw the power of music the day I sat in church, not conscious that I was wearing a very heavy heart. When the choir started singing, the song pierced me right to my bones and my eyes got so wet that I put my head down and used two tissues before the song was over. It has been said that "music is the language of the soul." When the melody and the words strike the right chord in someone's soul, the impact is profound. Pray for musicians to receive God's inspiration for both the message and the melody for maximum impact. The God of excellence will produce quality musicians for quality music.

Who the musician is also matters. Once I was on a bus, a video of a particular musician started playing and I realized I was getting angry. The music, though secular, was good and had a good message. However, because I knew a little about the man singing, the negative impact he has had on his family, and how he has frustrated some people, I found myself struggling to hear him. When David the great musician of God's temple sinned and God rebuked him through the Prophet Nathan, David wrote a song of repentance; Psalm 51. Among other things He cried out to God:

"Against you, you only, have I sinned and done what is evil in your sight; so you are right in your verdict and justified when you judge. Cleanse me with hyssop, and I will be clean; wash me, and I will be whiter than snow. Create in me a pure heart, O God, and renew a steadfast spirit within me. Do not cast me from your presence or take your Holy Spirit from me" (Psalm 51:4, 7, 10-11 NIV).

Today, encourage a musician or two and pray that:

- They will love and honor God in their lives and music.
- They will strive to live pure lives, above sin, so that the impact of their music will be much greater and their future in heaven sure.
- Their hearts will be filled with the right spirit; the Spirit of God, for spiritual impact; and
- They will remain in the presence of God always.

These are pillars for success in the music ministry.

Dearly Beloved, as you tune your heart to music, ensure that what you listen to is building your spirituality, drawing you into a meaningful life and taking you away from worldly passions. May the music you play glorify God and bless humanity. May the music you hear bring you closer to God and build you to bless humanity. Then, shall you be blessed, in Jesus' Name.

Day 90 *Praise & Celebration*

PLEASE THE GREATEST PLEASURE GIVER!

How is it that humanity easily gets distracted and deceived of the real source of pleasure? The innocent baby thinks that the breast is all he or she needs to be pleased. So, whatever happens, the mother's breast must bring some quietness before the baby realizes that the pain is not from hunger.

Shortly after, the baby believes that the only one that cares and can help is the mother. He wants no one else to carry him but the mother.

When teenage years come, close friends become the real source of pleasure in their brains. "You are to me like water to a desert dweller, the sugar in my tea, and the air I breathe," they would say. The parents know and can help very little, if at all. God is far from holding the key to their lives!

Soon they get into the professional age and their job becomes their god, or the fetish from a witch doctor becomes their source of comfort, safety, hope and good sales in their company.

Ah, at the height of pleasure and leisure, sports are a collective pleasure giver. They invite people out on Sunday morning and keep them up late at night, in the bar with a bottle of something to "quench the thirst," after all "pleasure" strains the shouting voice and weakens the jubilant body.

At old age, a person's god is the stick he can lean on, the children who provide his needs daily or the drugs he takes frequently to stay afloat.

But all these bracers on which humanity leans in tough times are only as effective as God makes them.

I watched a friend lose friends after losing out on his job. Even all the friends who gave advice, kept company in those hot pleasure days, loaned money for drinks, and accompanied him for sports, suddenly became unavailable and unable to help. I have seen men sobbing and lamenting: "Pastor, everyone has abandoned me, even my dear wife," as they struggled out amidst tears and saliva.

Beloved, as you spend time in the presence of the Lord, know that there is no better source of pleasure than God. Even when things are so bad and you are tempted to think that God does not remember that you exist, be like Habakkuk. After lamenting the pain of Israel in exile and complaining passionately, God's response let him conclude:

"Even though the fig trees have no blossoms, and there are no grapes on the vines; even though the olive crop fails, and the fields lie empty and barren; even though the flocks die in the fields, and the cattle barns are empty, yet I will rejoice in the Lord! I will be joyful in

the God of my salvation! The Sovereign Lord is my strength! He makes me as surefooted as a deer, able to tread upon the heights" (Habakkuk. 3:17-19 NLT).

He moved from complaint to composure when he realized that his real source of joy is neither people nor situations but God!

Whatever your situation and whoever may be loving you or fighting you, celebrate and please God, your ultimate pleasure giver. That is a way to bless and be blessed in a very deceptive world, in Jesus' Name.

Service

Day 91 — Service

SERVE TO SAVE LIVES!

"Mami, shift ahead. You sit to the back and you, brother, stand up a little. OK, good. Now, you enter and just stand up a little. Let me close the door, then you try to sit. Do not worry, if you do not sit well, brother will carry you. What is important is that we all go. OK, good. Let me close the door. Good! Now we can go!" This was the way we were loaded in vehicles in those days, so that six people could sit behind the driver instead of three. The driver sat with three others in front with the fourth on his left while he drove! Even though they insisted that it was so many would be able to travel, it was for the drivers to get some more money. Sometimes they also complained that they did that to have money for the police and gendarmes on the road and still be left with at least some profit. They did not think of the comfort, health and safety of their passengers. Self-centered service is one of those things destroying humanity.

It is easy to talk of the pastor as one working for the salvation of souls. It is easy to see that the medical doctor is there to save people from death, yet we have pastors who have become hunters from the pulpit instead of shepherds, and medical workers who have become blood suppliers to occultic kingdoms through the people they kill in practice! What a world!

Every service is God-ordained to save humanity. Teachers keep society advancing by producing brains that grow to invent, produce, and govern among others. The police and gendarmes are law-keepers meant to keep the society safe from lawbreakers, the cleaner in the office keeps healthy those who are allergic and the director-general saves the company from failure and enables it to effectively provide for a public that needs its services or products.

John the Baptist was in the Jordan preaching and baptizing people.

"Even tax collectors came to be baptized. 'Teacher,' they asked, 'what should we do?' 'Don't collect any more than you are required to,' he told them. Then some soldiers asked him, 'And what should we do?' He replied, 'Don't extort money and don't accuse people falsely - be content with your pay'" (Luke 3:12-14 NIV).

When Jesus visited Zacchaeus and his eyes opened to the truth, his repentance was marked by restitution:

"Zacchaeus stood up and said to the Lord, 'Look, Lord! Here and now I give half of my possessions to the poor, and if I have cheated anybody out of anything, I will pay back four times the amount.' Jesus said to him,

'Today salvation has come to this house, because this man, too, is a son of Abraham'" (Luke 19:8-9 NIV).

Beloved in the Lord, God has assigned you first, to serve and save lives spiritually and physically. In the process, God will provide for your needs. If you would serve to save lives rather than thinking of yourself and how you would benefit, be content with your pay and ask God to add to it in His own way. Remain faithful in saving as you serve. Do not let anyone that you are serving suffer or complain about you as selfish. Being a blessing to others through your work is the way to be blessed, in Jesus' Name.

Day 92 — Service

COMMITMENT MAKES EVERY AGE MEANINGFUL!

Do they say grey hair indicates wisdom? I know of a young person who had a lot of grey hair on his head; so much that one could think he was elderly if his young face did not betray him. It was and still is held by many that grey hair is a sign of old age and aging means getting wiser. True but at what age does the aging process bring in brain depreciation, thus less mental productivity? If age did not bring such a reduced capability of a person's ability to perform mentally, retirement would not make much sense.

When people go far beyond both retirement age and beyond the ability to think wisely because of tired brains, but still refuse to give way to fresh brains, there is a problem. Moses asked God to teach us to number our days and be wise. Numbering days entails two things:

- Being conscious of your days of productivity and making the most use of them. In this case, you make use of the days of your youth in serving God, your community and yourself. Indeed, the truth Jesus reminded Peter of applies to all human beings.
  "Very truly I tell you, when you were younger you dressed yourself and went where you wanted; but when you are old you will stretch out your hands, and someone else will dress you and lead you where you do not want to go" (John 21:18 NIV).

If in your young age you served nobody, in your days of old, you will have no one to hold your hand and lead you. And if in your old age your wisdom is not aiding the young, they will not be by you to help when you need younger eyes with which to see, younger hands with which to touch and hold, and younger brains with which to interpret reality. In the days of your youth, serve with strength and in the days of your agedness, serve humanity with your counsel.

- Fearing and serving your God. When you number your days, you know that the time you have on earth, long or short, is from the Lord. He promised, **"Then you will know that I am in Israel, that I am the Lord your God, and that there is no other; never again will my people be shamed. 'And afterward, I will pour out my Spirit on all people. Your sons and daughters will prophesy, your old men will dream dreams, your young men will see visions'"** (Joel 2:27-28 NIV).

There is a service a young person can do that the older person would not. There are services at experienced age that a young person would just destroy.

Beloved in the Lord, you number your days before a great God who knows why He takes some people early and allows others to live longer. At whatever age you are, seek His guidance and give God an appropriate service in an appropriate manner, and be blessed, in Jesus' Name.

Day 93   Service

DO NOT JUST LIVE TO "MAKE IT" IN LIFE!

When all is going well and attractive, a major focus of life is to make it; to achieve big things and be a great person. I followed a conversation between an elderly man and a young guitarist. "What do you want out of your life?" the old man asked. "I want to make it." the guitarist said. The old man said, "Do not live to make it." Then he walked away. The question is, when you have made it, then what?

Have you noticed that in the Western world most of those who "make it" establish foundations? It seems like they get up one day and realize that first, they do not need as much money as they have, and second, they are not impacting people with the money very much. So, they look for a channel through which they can get their wealth to say something better about them than just that they have made it in life. For a child of God, success is finding God's will and doing it. That means that life is not successful because you have accomplished some great thing, but because you have *done* the will of God for you.

Both from His example and in His calling us to love one another, God's value of us is in terms of how much difference we make in the lives of others. It was after Jesus was resurrected and accomplished His mission that He came to the disciples and, **"Again Jesus said, 'Peace be**

with you! As the Father has sent me, I am sending you'" (John 20:21 NIV). Note from the text:

- He left us peace as the greatest accomplishment in His life. Yes, if you consider "making it in life" as making a life-changing difference in the lives of others, the Lord will help you to make it in life.
- The order of living is defined by the Father. Jesus sends us into the world to live, work and impact others as the Father sent Him. The Father sent Him to serve and save in love, to teach and show the way to a meaningful life, and to destroy the works of Satan in all humanity. Our Father, His Father, has sent us to make a difference in the lives of others.

Solomon "made it" in life, big time! He built his magnificent palace and a great temple for God. His wisdom was known throughout the world of his time. He was famous but, it is David who, without a single building or any wealth to his credit, is most favored by God. Jesus comes in the linage of David, the man after God's heart. He knew God's will and did it. Would you want to be remembered as a David or a Solomon? If you just live to make it, you may make it and be a Solomon; rich and famous *only*. If you live to make others fulfilled, you will be remembered like David, blessed and blessing others. May that be your portion, in Jesus' Name.

Truth and Self-Control

Day 94   *Truth & Self-Control*

LIFE IS NOT A GAME!

The phrase "playing life" seems to be out of fashion today but was once very popular. It was used by or for people who lived a high-level of sensual fulfillment and were often proud of it. To such people, life was a game in which they changed players (girlfriends and boyfriends) and fields (moving from town to town or from one nightclub to another). The result was often separation from spouse, divorce, and poverty (such as bankruptcy or closure of business). At worst, it led to early death. While the phrase is not popular anymore, life is still a game to many. They live to eat, drink, have merry and then, die!

Your life is a game when all what you think about is the satisfaction of your emotions rather than the accomplishment of any purpose in your life. You do not care very much about tomorrow as long as you have something to eat and drink today and an opportunity to "enjoy yourself!" You do not ask yourself questions such as "When will I get married; what will happen to my children?" You just live! Any good that happens to you is by grace or chance because you never really planned; you just saw it happen.

Your life is a game when you can do anything to get what you want. You do not allow anyone to stand in your way. You push him or her away, sacrifice or kill, if necessary, to get money, promotion or recognition. This is the life that reigns in corruption and blood but often ends in tragedy.

Your life is a game if all that matters to you is success no matter how you get it. You destroy friendships, bribe left and right, belong to all kinds of societies with conflicting values, and/or sacrifice your integrity to get success. Students buy marks from their teachers with their bodies and teachers publish student research papers without acknowledging the students so that they can get promotion for work that is not theirs. You crush things or people and ride to wealth and fame on questionable means. That game could last long but at some point, you can become a very well-known unpopular person. Life can catch up very badly on you.

Dear friend, God did not bring you to earth to play life but to enjoy it in a proper way, make a difference in the lives of others and glorify the Name of God. He created you and brought you to earth to do good works. **"For we are God's handiwork, created in Christ Jesus to do good works, which God prepared in advance for us to do" (Ephesians 2:10 NIV).** The good work is in two phases:

- Believe in the Lord Jesus Christ. **"Jesus answered, 'The work of God is this: to believe in the one he has sent'" (John 6:29 NIV).**

- Do good to others. It will cost you but will also give you greater fulfillment and success in life. "**Live such good lives among the pagans that, though they accuse you of doing wrong, they may see your good deeds and glorify God on the day he visits us**" (1 Peter 2:12 NIV).

Success is knowing and doing God's will. That is the highway to changing your life from a game to a gain. That is the highway to being blessed. Take it and change the course of your life to the best; *from a game to a gain,* in Jesus' Name.

LIVE BY GRACE AND TRUTH

Although he was a baptized Christian, for some reason, he did not attend chapel in his Christian boarding school one day. The school authorities decided to look for him. He ran into the forest but was eventually caught. To get himself free, he told them he was actually a Muslim and gave them a Muslim name for himself. He was freed. He lived a lie in those days, and that fake Muslim name became his nickname for a while. Why did he not just tell the truth as to why he stayed away from the chapel? Why was he afraid of being punished for doing what was wrong? It takes God to live in the truth, because it takes grace to speak and live the truth.

A clear indication that someone is not a Christian is the absence of truth in his or her life. Jesus came to earth with two great things which He brought to us out of His love. **"The Word became flesh and made his dwelling among us. We have seen his glory, the glory of the one and only Son, who came from the Father, full of grace and truth" (John 1:14 NIV).**

He came full of grace and truth.

For lack of truth families are split. One person says something that has no true substance and sets the heart of the rest of the family members at loggerheads. For lack of truth a nation goes down the drain, as people in power give the impression that all is well. In reality, they are siphoning state funds into their private bank accounts and leaving hospitals, schools and other social services suffering, roads dilapidated and people dying of hunger in a world of abundance. For lack of truth people uplift themselves and behave bigger than they are.

"For by the grace given me I say to every one of you: Do not think of yourself more highly than you ought, but rather think of yourself with sober judgment, in accordance with the faith God has distributed to each of you" (Romans 12:3 NIV).

When you think of yourself more than you ought to, you live a standard of life above your means and become a debtor sooner or later, struggling to sustain a deceptive public image. It takes grace to take yourself as you are.

Grace and Truth reside in the person of Jesus Christ. He does not just teach the truth; He is the Truth Himself. And these three go together: Truth, Way, Life! There is no way to God without the truth and there is no life without God. Therefore, dear friend:

- Have Jesus as your personal Lord and Savior and you will graciously live in the truth. Then, your life will be more meaningful, more satisfying and you will be sure to enter heaven.
- Talk to people about Christ and encourage them to believe in Him. That is the way to bring unity in the

family and the way to bring change, life and sustainable development in the community or nation.

May the Lord help you to walk in the truth, in Jesus, and help others live in the truth for your life and for theirs, for your blessings and for theirs, in Jesus' Name.

Wealth

Day 96   Wealth

WHEN WEALTH BREEDS PRIDE!

One of the greatest results of wealth is pride. The wealthy who become proud see no more problems in life and no need for anything else, because money can do all things. Money is power! We saw this man grow up in a community where I lived. He became rather wealthy. Yes, he had business ideas and worked hard getting what he got. However, after some time he became the scorn of the community. He became well hated and was accused of getting into the spirit world of occultism to get even richer. His activities became bizarre, and he sponsored robbery and evil in the community because he was untouchable. Pride isolates from humanity but builds a friendship with exploiters. Pride isolates terribly from God.

When wealth breeds pride, it makes itself the goal of the owner's heart and pushes God aside, if He is even present at all. While the Bible teaches much about wealth and God promises to enrich, the Bible also warns against wealth taking the place of God. The story of the rich young ruler tells how wealth can replace God. The young man expressed a great desire to enter the Kingdom of God. He realized that being a law keeper was not enough. He had kept all the commandments in his understanding. Jesus told him to examine his heart, and he failed the test badly.

"When Jesus heard this, he said to him, 'You still lack one thing. Sell everything you have and give to the poor, and you will have treasure in heaven. Then come, follow me.' When he heard this, he became very sad, because he was very wealthy" (Luke 18:22-23 NIV).

When wealth makes one proud, it becomes the god of the person, leading not to joy but to isolation.

I recently read the story of a Kenyan who was very wealthy, had businesses and made money. God told him to sell all he had and take care of the orphans, street children and other lonely children. He did! We are told that he now has trained over ten thousand children who are in very gainful professions. He runs more than ten family centers in the nation. Is he not much richer than before? When wealth is spread into building people, giving life to others and making the community a better place to be, God empowers it, enriches the "rich" and is glorified.

Solomon realized how silly it was to have money, be proud enough to ignore God and see other human beings as insignificant. He experienced it and told us that all wealth without God is vanity upon vanity. His conclusion:

"Remember him - before the silver cord is severed, and the golden bowl is broken; before the pitcher is shattered at the spring, and the wheel broken at the

well, and the dust returns to the ground it came from, and the spirit returns to God who gave it. Now all has been heard; here is the conclusion of the matter: Fear God and keep his commandments, for this is the duty of all mankind" (Ecclesiastes 12:6-7, 13 NIV).

Beloved, let not wealth pridefully take your heart away from God. Let His blessings to you cause you to fear Him more; love Him more; invest in His Kingdom more; be humble before Him much more; build more humans for better living and be a great blessing in the communities in which God places you. Then, will God bless you even more and you will bless others likewise, in Jesus' Name.

WORSHIP GOD WITH YOUR WEALTH!

It makes a difference in God's Kingdom and means much in others' lives when people worship the Lord with their wealth. I can still see joy and beaming smiles on people's faces as a result of a medical mission we made seven to eight years ago to some very enclaved areas in Eastern Cameroon. People's lives have been transformed by others' testimonies who gave their time, money, and skills for the Lord. People pass our church and raise their voices to God in worship. It is because they have seen people worshipping God with their wealth, by investing in an edifice that lets people sit out of the rain and sun, to worship God in comfort. If, indeed, God is the giver of what you have, it makes sense that He should be the greatest receiver of what great things your wealth can do. That must be the mindset that led David to declare,

"But the king replied to Araunah, 'No, I insist on buying it, for I will not present burnt offerings to the Lord my God that have cost me nothing.' So David paid him fifty pieces of silver for the threshing floor and the oxen" (2 Samuel 24:24 NLT).

A few things can help you to worship God with your wealth.

- Check your heart. One's treasure follows his or her heart. There are people who do little about their struggling church but give huge amounts to political activities. Once a man falls in love, he spends more on that individual than he does on those around him. The story of Zacchaeus tells that one of the marks of heart transformation, salvation, is a God-glorifying use of wealth. The more you fall in love with God, the more you will worship Him with your wealth.

- See beyond the pastor. The greatest distraction in people giving to God has been a focus on the pastor. Some church people and even unchurched onlookers are vexed at the least comfort of pastors. They think that giving to the church is giving to pastors' comfort. Sadly, numerous charlatans have filled pulpits and "business centers" called churches, calling themselves men or women of God. They are both their congregation's pastors and treasurers and give account to no one! See the God of the food where you worship and receive your spiritual feeding, instead of concentrating on the pastor, the one who is holding the spoon and feeding you. Honor God, worship God with your wealth and pray that God may ensure a good use of it. God will answer your prayers and give wisdom to those who are struggling to do right and punish those who use His Name to exploit.
- See giving to God as an investment. There is no better place to invest than in the hands of the best Manager in the universe, the greatest Rewarder, and the most loving Friend who never cheats. Peter was genuine is his complaint and Jesus was also genuine in His answer.

- **"Then Peter spoke up, 'We have left everything to follow you!' 'Truly I tell you,' Jesus replied, 'no one who has left home or brothers or sisters or mother or father or children or fields for me and the gospel will fail to receive a hundred times as much in this present age: homes, brothers, sisters, mothers, children and fields - along with persecutions - and in the age to come eternal life'" (Mark 10:28-30 NIV).**
- All you have comes from God. When you give back to Him, you are investing. His reward comes in various ways including peace, fewer troubles in sicknesses and quarrels in your home or opened doors for you and yours.
- See God as your greatest treasure. Your greatest source of treasure is God from which all things come. We grew up in the village, carrying water from a stream for all domestic use. That source of our water received constant care from us. Once in two weeks or so, we cleaned it very well and provided a channel for overflow, so the water did not cause trouble around the area. If you can see God as the one in whom you live and move and have your being, you will not have any difficulty worshipping Him with your wealth.

Beloved in the Lord. God is the source of all good things. Make Him your treasure and your heart will never depart from Him. **"For where your treasure is, there your heart will be also" (Luke 12:34 NIV).** Worship Him with whatever He gives you out of love and care. God loves to give to you; care about His delight and worship Him with your wealth. You will certainly be more blessed and be a channel for blessing others, in Jesus' Name.

Day 98   *Wealth*

CELEBRATE THE LORD OF YOUR HARVEST

There is a part of me that greatly misses village life. I can see in my mind great dancing and people coming into the church during Harvest Thanksgiving time, carrying corn in various sizes, some in the hands, others in buckets, or small bags. Sugarcane, beans, chickens, cowpeas, and roasted corn were among the regular items on the offertory altar. Then came the sales. Here, there was some form of competition, with people bidding various prices and the highest bidder taking home the item. Harvest Thanksgiving in the village used to be a tempting time as well as some wealthy people planned and saved to buy at this time. Since all here sold by auction and few people were wealthy, things sold at church were far cheaper than the market price. The church became wiser and decided that some of the items collected that were not perishable would be kept and sold at the market price at the end of the Harvest Thanksgiving period. In that way, God would not be robbed, and the buyer would not cheat God. People gave with great excitement because they recognized that all they harvested came from God.

Such excitement characterized the atmosphere in Israel when David led them to give in preparation for the building of the Temple. It was a leaders-led giving and,

"They gave toward the work on the temple of God five thousand talents and ten thousand darics of gold, ten thousand talents of silver, eighteen thousand talents of bronze and a hundred thousand talents of iron. Anyone who had precious stones gave them to the treasury of the temple of the Lord in the custody of Jehiel the Gershonite. The people rejoiced at the willing response of their leaders, for they had given freely and wholeheartedly to the Lord. David the king also rejoiced greatly" (1 Chronicles 29:7-9 NIV).

Note the kind of things they gave. They were high-quality, precious things worthy of the God they served. Yes, for you to celebrate the God of your Harvest seriously:

- Remember that you belong to God. After the giving, David was amazed, lifted his voice, and asked the Lord, rhetorically, **"But who am I, and who are my people, that we should be able to give as generously as this" (1 Chronicles 29:14a NIV)?** Both the ability and the opportunity to give are from God and should be recognized as such. You can only joyfully give to the God you know.
- Remember that all you have comes from Him. While Satan may try to distract us with the focus on how we worked and made wealth for ourselves, David reminds us greatly in this chapter that all we have is from God. After the giving, David praised God, saying, **"Wealth and honor come from you; you are the ruler of all**

things. In your hands are strength and power to exalt and give strength to all" (1 Chronicles 29:12 NIV). Then He confessed such great truth that must always precede Harvest Thanksgiving or another giving at all; **"Lord our God, all this abundance that we have provided for building you a temple for your Holy Name comes from your hand, and all of it belongs to you"** (1 Chronicles 29:16 NIV). All you have belongs to God. You have nothing that God has not given you. You can only make wealth when God gives you the strength to do so. Appreciate Him.

Oh, ye blessed of the Lord! Appreciate Him for your harvest of salary, proceeds from your farm, good health, beautiful children, a great family and much more. You may not count all because you cannot name them all. Above all, what do you have that can measure up to the value of salvation, a place in heaven that God has given you? Nothing! Out of all you are and have, bring to God your dancing shoes, your voice, your Harvest Thanksgiving items throughout the year, and your joy-filled heart. Let us always celebrate the God of our Harvest, in Jesus' Name.

WEALTH AND HEAVEN!

Nothing makes wealth as worthless and meaningless as death. In the face of death, the amount, importance, and value of wealth are brought to zero. No amount, quality or value of wealth can buy life or stop death from coming to anyone. The rich or poor, the wise or foolish, the great or common, the free or slave, the oppressed or oppressor and the ruled and the ruler all die. Death is one of the greatest mysteries of life.

"...those who trust in their wealth and boast of their great riches? No one can redeem the life of another or give to God a ransom for them - the ransom for a life is costly, no payment is ever enough - so that they should live on forever and not see decay. For all can see that the wise die, that the foolish and the senseless also perish, leaving their wealth to others" (Psalm 49:6-10 NIV).

Given this reality, is it not more important to build a life and wealth that concentrates on the world beyond?

Yes, there is wealth that concentrates on the world beyond. Materialism, power and office, degrees and diplomas will not concentrate there.

"And I heard a voice from heaven saying, 'Write this down: Blessed are those who die in the Lord from now on. Yes, says the Spirit, they are blessed indeed, for

they will rest from their hard work; for their good deeds follow them!" (Revelation14:13 NLT). Two things:

- It is a blessing to die in the Lord. The Bible reminds us, when Jesus is not at the center of your heart, no matter how rich you are, you are poor and wretched. The presence of Christ in your heart:
    1) Ensures your entrance into eternal life, into heaven;
    2) Gives your earthly life both meaning and understanding, so the wealth you have is best used;
    3) Gives an eternal value to the good things you do on earth (with a godly motive).

Without Christ in you, the value of your wealth is purely physical and can even be destructive.

- Good deeds, good works, works that make the lives of others better and promote or expand the Kingdom of God, is what counts in eternity. It is these good works that will follow you to eternity.

Beloved in the Lord, God has not given you wealth to pave your way to hell with a combination of pride, wickedness or exploitation that wealth often brings to some people. God has given you wealth so that you can make a great difference in the lives of others and expand His Kingdom. If you are still looking for wealth, may your objective be the advancement of Christ's Kingdom among humankind. When Christ is at the center of your heart and will, eternal value will be at the center of your wealth, heaven and earth will rejoice that you are wealthy, and God will bless you more as you bless others, in Jesus' Name.

Day 100   Your Response

WHEN TIME DIES WHERE WILL YOU BE?

People often think that they can plan and execute things in their own time and at their own pace when it is not in their ability to decide or control the events of their lives. The reality is that time will pass one day and eternity will take over. At that "time" we will lose count of time. For the saved, **"The sun will no more be your light by day, nor will the brightness of the moon shine on you, for the Lord will be your everlasting light, and your God will be your glory" (Isaiah 60:19 NIV).** Time will pass away; you will enter eternity. However, where shall you be, and in what situation? Beauty or beaten, proud or in pain, happy or hunting for water, heaven or hell? Now is the time for you to make a choice. There is no escape and delays may be dangerous.

We were classmates and "Njok", greatly "enjoyed" life. He was very handsome and intelligent, and girls flocked after him. He mocked our going to church and trying to be disciplined. His father might have been giving him money, or else he stole from him, because he spent money freely and the night club was his home away from home. Yes, he still passed his GCE examination which gave him another reason to be even more proud. Looking now at the signs and symptoms of what took him to the grave, I believe he got HIV and AIDS and died a few weeks after the results were released. It was painful, yet not surprising. He did not hold his life in his hands as he thought he did!

Beloved, if you have not given your life to Jesus Christ, you are free to continue to argue and comfort yourself with:

- *"I still have time. I am young."* Have you not seen young people die unexpectedly? Why will your case be different? You can only comfortably confess, "I will not die young" if you can finish with, "In Jesus' Name," but saying that without Jesus in your heart means nothing.
- *"There is nothing like hell because God is love and cannot throw those made in His image into hell fire."* However, remember that punishment is never too heavy when you know the consequences before you go astray. A God of justice cannot lay aside justice for love. In fact, love compels Him to be just; justice demands punishment, and hell or heaven are just a fulfillment of a promise He has made to those He loves. He has loved you enough to tell you now that hell exists. It is your choice to escape it or not.
- *"God does not even exist, so I have nothing to worry about."* Really? Instead of asking someone to prove to you that God exists, prove for yourself that He does not. Before you point to the problem of evil and tell me of God's inability to stop evil, let me remind you that

    1) God warned about the emergence and danger of evil before Adam and Eve sinned.

2) God gives an ultimate solution to evil.

Just look at two families in your neighborhood. Those who live in love have no evil among them. Their lives are great. Those who hate each other live with evil and even fear one another. Love in its best form is from God as a solution to evil. Jesus died to make that love possible.

Before you get too comfortable with science over Christianity, please explain the origin of

1) The material that exploded in the "big bang" to give rise to life; and

2) The source and nature of the force that made that material explode!

- *"Christianity does not work; Christians are unable to overcome sin."* However, remember that Jesus Christ did not die for the whole but the one in the whole. That is what it means when we say salvation is personal. Christianity is a process, not an accomplishment. Do not forget the charlatans of faith whose god is their stomach, and their end is destruction. They even dwell in churches and on pulpits. So, **"... Fixing our eyes on Jesus, the pioneer and perfecter of faith. For the joy set before him, he endured the cross, scorning its shame, and sat down at the right hand of the throne of God"** (Hebrews 12:2a NIV). Jesus showed by example that life can be lived right. He died to kill the power that disables righteous living and promises to be there to help those who want to live right. For real Christians, Christ lives in and for them.

Dear friend, you are able to resist God because He has given you free will. You are not a robot, and He does not control you with a remote-control. He has told you that hell awaits those who turn their backs on Him. What if you run away from Him and discover at death that He is really who the Bible says He is? He has told you that He can make life great for you if you trust in Him.

Accept you have sinned.

Believe Christ died for you.

Confess your sins with repentance.

Depend on Him for your daily walk in righteousness; and

Expect great things from Him for He will indeed do great things for you. Time will elapse, eternity will take over. Where you will be is your choice. Choose wisely; Choose Christ, and be blessed, in Jesus' Name.

Appendix

Names in "" are pseudonyms to protect the identity of people.

Many cultural and regional phrases have been retained to give flavor to Rev. Nfor's life in Cameroon. As Rev. Nfor has lived throughout the world, some words and phrases reflect world-wide language diversity.

Devotions are taken from Rev. Nfor's original Pacesetter postings.

About the Author

MA of Agricultural & Political Economics, University of Aberdeen, Scotland (1991)

Worked as agro-economist, Ministry of Agriculture, Cameroon

Master of Divinity in Theology, Ogbomoso, Nigeria

Doctor of Ministry, leadership emphasis, North American Baptist Seminary, Sioux Falls, South Dakota, USA

Professor: Cameroon Baptist Theological Seminary, Ndu

Dean of International Leadership, University, Yaoundé, Cameroon

Pastoral Ministry: Etoug-Ebe Baptist Church (2007-2016)

Church Planting & Senior Pastor: Patmos Baptist Church 2017-present, (Yaoundé, Cameroon)

Born: Ntumbaw. Rev. Nfor lives in Yaoundé, Cameroon

www.ingramcontent.com/pod-product-compliance
Lightning Source LLC
Chambersburg PA
CBHW071303110426
42743CB00042B/1152